Fodor's

GAY GUIDE

TO

san francisco

AND THE BAY AREA

BY ANDREW COLLINS

FODOR'S TRAVEL PUBLICATIONS, INC.

NEW YORK • TORONTO • LONDON • SYDNEY • AUCKLAND

HTTP://WWW.FODORS.COM/

Fodor's Gay Guide to San Francisco and the Bay Area

Editor: Daniel Mangin
Editorial Contributors: Steven K. Amsterdam, Glen Berger, Kaline J. Carter, Steve Crohn, Janet Foley, James Sinclair
Map Editor: Robert P. Blake
Creative Director: Fabrizio La Rocca
Cartographer: David Lindroth, Inc.; Eureka Cartography
Cover Design: Allison Saltzman
Text Design: Between the Covers

Copyright

Special Sales

CONTENTS

Maps

AUTHOR'S NOTE

BEING GAY OR LESBIAN influences our choice of accommodations, nightlife, dining, shopping, and perhaps even sightseeing. This book will enable you to plan your trip confidently and with authority. On the following pages I've tried to provide ideas for every segment of our community, giving you the skinny on everything from bars and clubs to gay beaches, from where to find a comprehensive feminist bookstore in Oakland to the best Thai food in the Castro. You'll also find a wide selection of accommodations, from exclusively lesbian or gay resorts to mainstream hotels.

About Me

I'm a gay male in my late twenties. I grew up in Connecticut, graduated from Wesleyan University, have lived briefly in London and Atlanta, and currently divide my time between a small house in New Hampshire's Monadnock mountains and an apartment in New York City's East Village.

How I Researched This Book

I've made several trips to San Francisco and the Bay Area over the past few years; most recently I spent three months driving up and down the West Coast, crashing on friends' sofas and testing out dozens of hotels and guest houses. At every stop I interviewed gays and lesbians—newspaper editors, activists, barflies, and people on the street—to get the latest scoop.

This is an opinionated book. I don't hesitate to say what I think—I'm prone to describe certain neighborhoods as characterless, resorts as touristy or uppity, restaurants as dumpy or over-the-top. My intention is always to relate what I've observed and what I've heard locals say.

For the most part I travel without announcing myself—the majority of the businesses in this book had no idea I was writing about them when I visited. In the end *Fodor's Gay Guide to San Francisco and the Bay Area* is a service not to hotels and guest houses, or to gay bars and restaurants, or to anybody in the travel industry. It is a resource for you, the traveler.

Language and Voice

I've written this book in a casual, personal voice, using terms such as "faggy," "dyke," and "queer" the way my friends and I do in general conversation. I know that for some people these words are painful reminders of more repressive times—be assured that no offense is intended. Also, unless the context suggests otherwise, when I use the terms "gay" or "homosexual," I'm referring to gay men and lesbians. I specify gender only as needed for clarity.

Content

Each chapter is divided into several sections. Here's a quick rundown of the major ones:

The Lay of the Land

If you're looking for a quick summation of each destination's geography, its neighborhoods and major attractions, and its shopping, you'll want to read this carefully. At the end are tips on getting around.

Eats

I'm a restaurant junkie, so I've included a broad range of options. The places I investigated were suggested by gay and lesbian locals, advertise in gay publications, or have received positive reviews in local newspapers and magazines. I stopped by almost every restaurant (and ate at as many as I could) to study the menu, check out the decor and ambience, and observe the crowd.

I've tried to include choices for every budget. Many recommendations are in or near gay-oriented neighborhoods. A few establishments get a nod less for the food than the overtly festive atmosphere. Conversely, some places are listed because they represent some of the destination's finest or

most unusual dining. The omission of your personal favorite may be more because it was similar to a place I did review than because I think it's not up to snuff. Unless otherwise noted, any restaurant in this book is at least somewhat popular with the community.

The Eats section ends with a sampling of area coffeehouses. Unless there's a description of the fare, assume that only light snacks and coffee are served.

The following chart explains the price categories for restaurants in this guide:

CATEGORY	COST*
$$$$	over $20
$$$	$15–$20
$$	$9–$15
$	under $9

*cost of dinner entrée

Scenes

I checked out nearly every bar within a two-hour drive of San Francisco. If a place opened after my visit to the area, I telephoned an employee and also got a report from a knowledgeable local resource to ensure an accurate review.

The most popular spots are listed under the heading "Prime Suspects," and are also located with bullets on the dining maps. I've also written short reviews about neighborhood bars, roving parties, and sporadic events—plus a few straight bars with queer-friendly reputations.

Male-oriented places outnumber those that cater to women by about 10 to 1. This is not a reflection of my preferences but of America's gay-bar culture—it's overwhelmingly young and male. Still, don't assume that a bar described as 80% male or mostly young doesn't welcome lesbians or older guys. Descriptions of each bar's crowd and its "cruise factor" are based on my observations and interviews and are provided simply to give you a profile of what's typical.

Under the heading "Action," I've listed a few bathhouses, adult theaters, and the like. I'd be remiss if I didn't tell you what's where. (I would also be remiss if I didn't encourage you to play safely and observe local regulations.)

Sleeps

In most chapters I've included gay-specific establishments that I felt confident recommending. I visited most of the B&Bs and small inns (usually anonymously), though I stayed in only a handful. If the establishment was straight-owned and I had no knowledge of its gay-friendliness, I checked with the owners to verify their interest in being covered in a gay publication. My descriptions of the clientele, compiled without the owners' input, are there to give you a general sense of the place.

When I discuss larger hotels, particularly those in cities, don't assume that they are gay-friendly (or otherwise) unless the reviews specifically state so. Obviously the degree of tolerance you encounter at a large property with many employees will depend largely on who happens to assist you. I included both mainstream properties that are in and near gay neighborhoods and those that have a strong reputation within the community.

The following chart explains the price categories used for lodging establishments in this guide:

CATEGORY	COST*
$$$$	over $180
$$$	$130–$180
$$	$90–$130
$	under $90

cost of double-occupancy room in high season

The Little Black Book

This is your quick resource guide for every destination. If some establishments have closed by the time you read about them—bars and restaurants are unpredictable—try the contacts here to get the latest info. Local tourist boards can be helpful, and lesbigay bookstores and community centers are tremendous resources. I've included a few gay-popular gyms, and the phone numbers of resources for persons who are HIV-positive or who have AIDS.

Disclaimer

This is where I'm to remind you that time brings changes, and that neither I nor Fodor's can accept responsibility for errors. An incredible amount of time and effort has been spent ensuring the accuracy of this book's information, but businesses move and/or close and restaurants and bars change. Always call an establishment before you go to make sure that it will be open when you get there.

The mention of any business, attraction, or person in this book is in no way an indication of sexual orientation or attitudes about sexual orientation. Unless specifically stated, no business in this book is implied or assumed to be gay-owned or -operated.

Send Letters

Whatever your reaction to this book—delight, excitement, unbridled rage—your feedback is greatly appreciated. I'd love to hear about your experiences, both good and bad, and about establishments you'd like me to include or exclude in future editions. Send your letters to me c/o Fodor's Travel Publications, 201 East 50th Street, New York, NY 10022, or e-mail me at gayfodors@aol.com.

In the meantime, I hope you'll have as much fun using this guide as I had writing it.

Andrew Collins

Andrew Collins
February 1997

Acknowledgments

I've been helped immeasurably by my editor, Daniel Mangin, a senior editor at Fodor's who's better known in the community as a film critic and teacher, a gossip columnist for the *Bay Area Reporter,* and for his gays-in-the-cinema film-clip show *Psycho Killers and Twisted Sisters.* His expertise in the spheres of travel and queer culture are in evidence throughout this book.

Many Bay Area residents shared their insights and opinions with me. Michelle Bouchard allowed me to crash on her fold-out sofa for more than a month, accompanied me on numerous bar runs, ate with me everywhere, and in general kept me out of serious trouble—for this I am eternally grateful. I'm also grateful to the following: Ty Accornero, Chris Arrott, Stephen Barber, Bertram in San Francisco, Mark Breckenridge, Sonya Bradley at the San Jose Convention and Visitors Bureau, Mary Casiano, Chip Conley and Rob Delamater of Joie de Vivre Hotels, Daryl from A Hole in the Wall, Robert Frankl, Peter Ian Cummings at *XY Magazine,* Glenn Dixon at the Highland Dell, Gabriel in Berkeley, Julie at the Cooper Street Cafe in Santa Cruz, Penny in Santa Cruz, Tom Pucci, Judith Rowcliffe, Chase Schade.

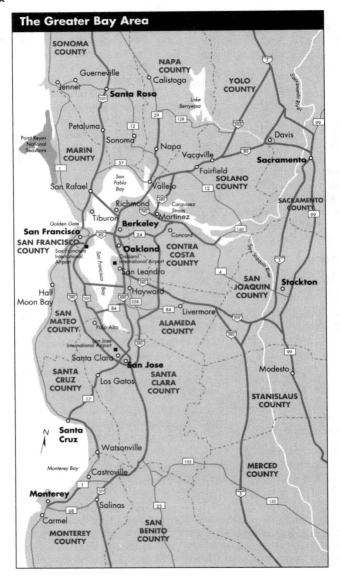

The Greater Bay Area

1 *Out in San Francisco*

PUNCTUATED BY HILLS, consumed by an eerie blanket of summer fog, and rarely marred by freezing temperatures, San Francisco is adored for its natural setting and its moderate climate. But a city is only as engaging as its inhabitants, and San Francisco's diverse ethnic makeup, its celebration of nonconformity, and its cerebral personality make it one of the world's most memorable metropolises.

Clichéd as it may sound, San Francisco is *the* gay mecca. Much of what draws gays and lesbians—outstanding performing and visual arts, world-class restaurants, sophisticated shopping, and a manageable layout—makes it a hit with everybody. A case could be made that San Francisco's attractions are more adult-oriented than other hot tourist locations such as Florida and southern California. Relatively few queerfolk travel with families, after all. But there's more to it than that.

Gay ghettos and entertainment districts have historically sprung up in cities' more licentious sections, so it should come as no surprise that a vibrant community evolved in what was arguably the "loosest" town in America, at least during the city's first few decades. New England's settlers were puritan—San Francisco's were anything but.

Northern California boomed in 1850 following the discovery of gold in the nearby Sierra foothills and, shortly thereafter, a rich vein of silver in Virginia City, Nevada. During the first 10 years of the gold rush San Francisco's population rose from 25,000 to about 350,000 inhabitants. Among the new arrivals were scrappy prospectors, rough-edged sailors, and other less than conventional spirits. Though vigilante justice reared its head from time to time, those living here learned to tolerate shady behavior in their fellow citizens. Gangsters and cheats ran the city, and brothels, saloons, and gaming houses flourished along Pacific Avenue from Sansome Street to Grant Avenue (called Dupont Street in the old days). As the 19th century drew to a close, this district, known as the Barbary Coast, averaged a murder a week. There aren't many recorded accounts of homosexual life in San Francisco during this era, but gays were definitely part of the landscape. Newspaper stories about the late-19th-century murder of a society matron, for instance, make it fairly clear that the initial suspect, later exonerated, was a gay man.

In 1906 the great earthquake and subsequent fire destroyed much of San Francisco, including the Barbary Coast (nowadays the comparatively dull Financial District). Moral conservatives considered the disaster a judgment from the heavens. "San Francisco Punished!" taunted the headline of a Los Angeles newspaper days after the quake, a sentiment echoed in the proclamations of modern-day fundamentalists in an entirely different, though no less venomous, context.

Fewer "depraved" operations thrived in the post-quake era, and most of these had been shut down by 1917. But San Francisco continued to lure sailors and thugs, as well as actors and musicians (the social good-for-nothings of the time). In early-20th-century accounts the town is frequently dubbed one of the "gayest" places in America—though the word "gay" at that time had little to do with same-sex orientation.

During World War II San Francisco was the point from which many naval enlistees sailed for Pacific tours of duty. The city swelled with men, and the Polk Gulch neighborhood became known for its male hustlers and covertly gay establishments. At about this time, and also largely because of the military presence, discreet lesbian clubs began to pop up.

The mid-'50s marked the beginning of two tumultuous decades of lesbian and gay-male activism. In 1955 the nation's first major lesbian political organization, the Daughters of Bilitis (DOB), was formed here under the leadership of Del Martin and Phyllis Lyon. Several mostly male-oriented homophile organizations also date from this period. Gays had made sufficient progress by 1959 to provoke the conservative *San Francisco Progress* to whine that "sex deviates" had turned the city into the nation's homosexual "headquarters." Gay and lesbian bars became more commonplace, though their owners had to pay off police to remain in business.

The forces of repression by no means ceased operations, however. At a 1965 ball sponsored by several gay political organizations, members of the San Francisco Police Department (SFPD) attempted to harass the roughly 600 attendees. When two gay lawyers and two straight bystanders stepped up to prevent the officers from pushing through the event, the four were handcuffed and tossed in jail. The American Civil Liberties Union defended those who were arrested, the mainstream press denounced the police force's actions, and the defendants were found innocent.

Chided for its strong-arm tactics, the SFPD struck back. To convince the public of the "tremendous threat" posed by the city's homosexuals, the department announced that as many as 70,000 gays and lesbians lived in San Francisco. Even local homos had a hard time believing the number was that large. The publicity spread rapidly, and the result was ironic: If you were a young "deviant" living elsewhere in America, you suddenly knew to pack your bags and move to San Francisco.

Up until this time Polk Street had been the main gay neighborhood, although a queer subset of the Beat Generation had established itself in North Beach. Lesbians, despite the success of the DOB, never ghettoized in San Francisco—gay women lived all over, making their presence seem less pronounced. Greater concentrations of lesbians could be found in nearby Berkeley and Oakland, where the feminist movement was gaining momentum.

In the early '70s the mostly Irish working-class Castro neighborhood evolved into one of the world's most recognizable gay ghettos. A smattering of gay men, among them the outspoken political activist Harvey Milk, who opened a camera shop on Castro Street, began to settle here. A tidal wave of gay-male—mostly white and middle-class—immigration followed. In Edmund White's *States of Desire,* David Goodstein, the former publisher of the *Advocate,* described the Castro of the late '70s as "essentially a refugee culture made up of gay men, who, in a sense, are convalescing in the ghetto from all of those damaging years in Podunk."

Indeed many Castro pilgrims were born in Podunk—Podunk, Georgia; Podunk, Ohio; Podunk, Utah; and so on. The

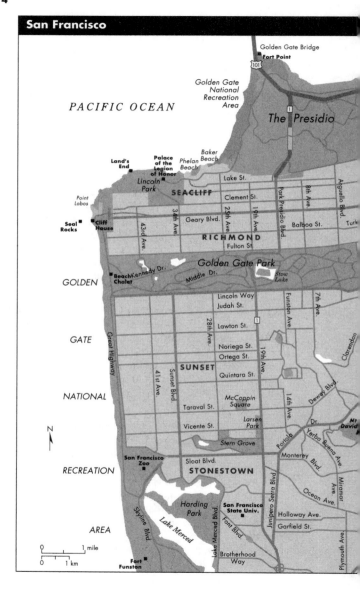

San Francisco

Golden Gate Bridge
Fort Point

Golden Gate National Recreation Area

PACIFIC OCEAN

The Presidio

Baker Beach

Land's End

Palace of the Legion of Honor

Phelan Beach

Lincoln Park

Lake St.

SEACLIFF

Clement St.

Point Lobos

Geary Blvd.

Park Presidio Blvd.

8th Ave.

Arguello Blvd.

Balboa St.

Turk

Seal Rocks

Cliff House

43rd Ave.

34th Ave.

RICHMOND

Fulton St.

25th Ave.

19th Ave.

Golden Gate Park

GOLDEN

Beach Chalet

Kennedy Dr.

Middle Dr.

Stow Lake

Lincoln Way

Judah St.

Funston Ave.

7th Ave.

GATE

28th Ave.

Lawton St.

Noriega St.

Ortega St.

19th Ave.

Clarendon

SUNSET

Quintara St.

NATIONAL

41st Ave.

Sunset Blvd.

McCoppin Square

Dewey Blvd.

Taraval St.

14th Ave.

Vicente St.

Larsen Park

Dr.

Mt David

Stern Grove

Portola

Yerba Buena

N

Monterey Blvd.

Miramar

RECREATION

San Francisco Zoo

Sloat Blvd.

STONESTOWN

Junipero Serra Blvd.

Ocean Ave.

Ave.

Harding Park

San Francisco State Univ.

Holloway Ave.

Garfield St.

Plymouth Ave.

AREA

Skyline Blvd.

Lake Merced

Lake Merced Blvd.

Font Blvd.

0   1 mile
0   1 km

Fort Funston

Brotherhood Way

Great Highway

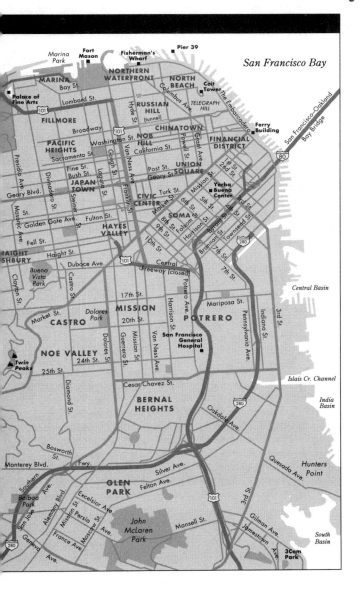

Marina Park • Fort Mason • Fisherman's Wharf • Pier 39

San Francisco Bay

NORTHERN WATERFRONT

MARINA
Bay St.

Palace of Fine Arts

NORTH BEACH • Coit Tower

Columbus Ave.

Lombard St.

TELEGRAPH HILL

FILLMORE

101

RUSSIAN HILL (tunnel)

Hyde St.

The Embarcadero

Broadway

101

CHINATOWN

San Francisco–Oakland Bay Bridge

PACIFIC HEIGHTS

Washington St.

NOB HILL

Ferry Building

Van Ness Ave.

California St.

Grant Ave.

Powell St.

FINANCIAL DISTRICT

Sacramento St.

Gough St.

80

Presidio Ave.

Fine St.
Bush St.

Post St.
Geary St.

UNION SQUARE

2nd St.

Geary Blvd.

Divisadero St.

JAPAN TOWN

Laguna St.

Steiner St.

Mission St.

Yerba Buena Center

3rd St.

Franklin St.

CIVIC CENTER

Turk St.

5th St.
6th St.

4th St.

St.

Golden Gate Ave.

Fulton St.

Market St.

SOMA

Masonic Ave.

HAYES VALLEY

Fell St.

Folsom St.

Harrison St.

Bryant St.

HAIGHT ASHBURY

Haight St.

10th St.

Brannan St.

Townsend St.

7th St.

Buena Vista Park

Dubace Ave.

Central Freeway (closed)

101

7th St.

280

Clayton St.

Castro St.

Potrero Ave.

Central Basin

Market St.

17th St.

Dolores Park

MISSION

Harrison St.

Mariposa St.

Pennsylvania Ave.

Indiana St.

3rd St.

CASTRO

20th St.

POTRERO

San Francisco General Hospital

NOE VALLEY

Dolores St.

Guerrero St.

Mission St.

Van Ness Ave.

Islais Cr. Channel

Twin Peaks

24th St.

25th St.

Diamond St.

Cesar Chavez St.

India Basin

BERNAL HEIGHTS

280

Oakdale Ave.

Bosworth St.

Quesada Ave.

Hunters Point

Monterey Blvd.

Fwy.

Silver Ave.

GLEN PARK

Felton Ave.

3rd St.

Southern

Balboa Park

Alemany Blvd.

San Jose Ave.

Excelsior Ave.

Mission St.

Persia St.

Moscow St.

France Ave.

John McLaren Park

Mansell St.

101

Gilman Ave.

Jamestown Ave.

South Basin

280

Geneva Ave.

3Com Park

so-called "Castro Street clone" typically waited tables, worked behind sales counters, or collected unemployment benefits. He partied a great deal and had plenty of sex with many partners. Thousands of young, often disaffected gay men bonded and, perhaps for the first time, felt that they were part of a much grander picture. Away from nonsupportive parents and siblings, they formed strong new family ties.

A crisis in 1978 further unified the Castro. Dan White, a disgruntled former city supervisor, assassinated San Francisco's gay-friendly mayor, George Moscone, and supervisor Harvey Milk—who had risen to become the state's first openly gay elected official. On May 21, 1979, White was convicted of manslaughter, courtesy of the famous "Twinkie defense" (that too much junk food had impaired his mental capacity), which carried a maximum sentence of just under eight years in prison—for murdering *two* city officials—with parole possible after five. That evening thousands of angry gays protested the lenient punishment on the steps of City Hall. They left behind about a million dollars in damage, including 11 burned police cars and hundreds of smashed windows. The following night the San Francisco police marched along Castro Street, yanking patrons from gay bars and beating them up. One bar, the Elephant Walk, later sued the city for damages and won. After serving several years in prison, White was released and committed suicide the next year.

In the 1980s the AIDS epidemic hit the city hard—mid-decade estimates put the number of HIV-positive men in the Castro district at above 50 percent. Opinions vary as to the long-term effects that the disease has had on the character and personality of the once-bacchanalian neighborhood. Clearly, life became dramatically more subdued during the '80s, and while the Castro is presently enjoying rejuvenation and a renewed trendiness, the place is not what it once was—though medical advances have made life easier for people with AIDS, the disease's role in daily life here is still evident.

On the plus side, the Castro is more diverse than before. People of all colors and classes now settle here, as do many lesbians. By the same token, more gays and lesbians live elsewhere around the city. Perhaps most significant is the emergence of the nation's most visible and powerful lesbian community, which has grown up right beside the Castro, in the lively Mission District.

Lesbians, whose voices were for so many years denied a serious platform, have become organized and vocal. The community supports woman-owned retail shops and restaurants, along with several performance spaces. Tension has always existed between San Francisco's gay men and lesbians—the type of "old-boy" network that often prevented qualified women from advancement in mainstream society operated similarly in the queer community. Tragically, AIDS took the lives of many men who had been at the forefront of San Francisco's gay movement. Lesbians not only picked up the slack, but often grabbed the reins and took charge. In the last decade, four different lesbians have held seats on the San Francisco Board of Supervisors.

The lesbian community has dedicated itself not only to its own advancement, but through volunteer work, fund-raising, and political lobbying has also participated in the fight against AIDS—even though few lesbians have contracted HIV and despite the fact that many of the men they have helped had previously held women in low regard. This compassionate response obviously reflects favorably on the women's community, but it also indicates that, the well-documented political and social divisions notwithstanding, the ties between lesbians and gay men here also run deep.

San Francisco strengthened its claim on the title of gayest city in America in late 1996 when the Board of Supervisors passed a regulation that requires all companies and organizations doing business with the city to provide domestic-partner benefits to their employees. As we were heading to press in early 1997, there was some grumbling in the corporate and religious communities, but the supervisors and Mayor Willie Brown were standing firm.

THE LAY OF THE LAND

Ringed to the east and north by San Francisco Bay and to the west by the Pacific Ocean, San Francisco sits at the northern tip of a peninsula. The city's terrain is hilly, and the land to the south and across the bay is downright mountainous—wherever you go, you're rarely without spectacular views of human and natural engineering. Within the city limits you'll find many small landscaped parks, as well as two large ones, the Presidio and Golden Gate Park.

San Francisco's busiest sections—the Financial District and Union Square (both of which form the heart of the city's downtown), North Beach, Chinatown, Nob Hill, and the waterfront—lie in its northeastern quadrant. South of here are mostly light-industrial and working-class neighborhoods, the nearest of which, SoMa (as in "South of Market" Street), underwent major urban renewal during the past three decades and resurfaced as a cultural center. West of downtown—from Pacific Heights clear out to the Richmond and Sunset districts—is more residential. Southwest of downtown, the old working-class immigrant neighborhoods such as the Mission District, Noe Valley, and the Castro, have become anywhere from a quarter to half gay and lesbian over the years.

The Castro

The gay community's hub is bounded roughly by Duboce Avenue to the north, Church Street to the east, 21st Street to the south, and Douglass Street to the west, though the surrounding territory is heavily queer as well. The main commercial activity fans out from the intersection of **Castro, 17th,** and **Market** streets to the east and south.

Since the early 1990s the Castro has diversified. Hip straights have bought property, and more curiosity-seekers are popping by (many of them on the F-line antique trolleys that now connect the Castro and downtown). Smart boutiques have opened up alongside many new restaurants. A new generation of young queers has melded in amazingly well with the longtime residents who saw the neighborhood through tough times. It's once again exciting to wander along Market Street and check out the buzz of commerce, cruising, and conversation.

The dining scene here was notoriously lame for many years, but Market Street from Castro Street east toward Van Ness Avenue has emerged as a culinary hot spot. It remains an easy place to find cheap diner food and ethnic cuisine.

Gay-oriented businesses along Market, 18th, and Castro streets continue to thrive, but new ones are attracting a broader mix of customers. Some favorites include **A Different Light** (⊠ 489 Castro St., ☎ 415/431–0891), the main lesbigay bookstore; **Under One Roof** (⊠ 2362 Market St., ☎

415/252–9430), which sells gifts and T-shirts to benefit AIDS organizations; **All American Boy** (⊠ 463 Castro St., ☎ 415/861–0444), an emporium of faggy fashion; the **Bead Store** (⊠ 417 Castro St., ☎ 415/861–7332), a repository of more than 1,000 types of beads; **Kozo** (⊠ 531 Castro St., ☎ 415/ 621–0869), an importer and maker of specialty papers, frames, and tchotchkes from the Far East and elsewhere; **Jaguar** (⊠ 4057 18th St., ☎ 415/863–4777), home to a luscious sampling of sex toys, novelties, lube, and greeting cards; **Wild Card** (⊠ 3979-B 17th St., ☎ 415/626–4449), known for trinkets and clever greeting cards; **Louie's Barber Shop** (⊠ 422 Castro St., ☎ 415/552–8472), a plain ole hair-cuttin' place frequented by plain ole dykes; **Does Your Mother Know...** (⊠ 4079 18th St., ☎ 415/864–3160), a homo take on a Hallmark store; the **Harvest Ranch Market** (⊠ 2285 Market St., ☎ 415/626–0805), a well-stocked gourmet and organic market that doubles as a lesbian pickup spot (don't take our word for it, see for yourself); and **Rolo** (⊠ 2351 Market St., ☎ 415/431–4545; ⊠ 450 Castro St., ☎ 415/861–1999), an emporium of Doc Martens, clubby designer clothing, and high-end grunge gear.

Architecturally the Castro is undistinguished in some areas and charmingly Victorian in others. The spectacular 1922 **Castro Theatre** (⊠ 429 Castro St., ☎ 415/621–6120) hosts the city's well-attended lesbian and gay film festival each summer; at other times it books first-run art films and many revivals. Films like *Who's Afraid of Virginia Woolf* or *Valley of the Dolls* take on a whole new interactive dimension when viewed with the Castro's audience, which supplements the audio track with campy renditions of choice lines. The balcony at this marvelous 1,500-seat Spanish Baroque landmark is, according to local lore, a great place to make out; so is the parking lot beside the theater.

Harvey Milk Plaza, above the Castro Muni Metro Station at Market and Castro streets, was dedicated in 1985. The plaque here has a moving inscription. The **Names Project Foundation** (⊠ 2362-A Market St., ☎ 415/863–1966) has a visitor center and panel-making workshop. The AIDS Memorial Quilt, begun here in 1987, consists of more than 40,000 hand-sewn panels, each a tribute created by the loved ones of a person who has fallen to AIDS. You can come here to make your own panel (materials and encouragement are provided) or to view some of the quilt's newer additions. People stop in from all over the world; for many it's part of a lengthy healing process.

Hello Gorgeous!! (✉ 549-A Castro St., ☎ 415/864–2628), a full-blown tribute to the career and celebrity of Barbra Streisand, takes its name from the opening line of the film *Funny Girl*. The store-gallery-museum is without question the Castro's most unusual attraction, but though this enterprise packs plenty of camp value, owner Ken Joachim has worked hard to create a serious appreciation of Barbra's work, filling the space with movie posters, memorabilia, and paintings of the singer-actress-director. Streisand mannequins wear outfits from her various films. If you're the type who believes that imitation is the sincerest from of flattery, you can get a makeover that will transform you—complete with wig and nose—into Babs herself. There's also an espresso bar that serves Jewish pastries. As yet, Barbra hasn't scheduled a visit, but she did send her best wishes.

Barbra wanna-bes and other queer talents take the stage at **Josie's Cabaret and Juice Joint** (✉ 3583 16th St., ☎ 415/861–7933), an authentic Castro institution that's a veggie café by day (*see* Eats, *below*) and by night (*see* Scenes, *below*) a showcase for such local and national luminaries as Lypsinka, Lea Delaria, Marga Gomez, and Tim Miller. The Pomo Afro Homos honed their performance pieces here before taking them very successfully on the road.

A great way to see the Castro is on the 3½-hour walking tour **Cruisin' the Castro** (☎ 415/550–8110), given by Trevor Hailey. She's a delightful speaker and a walking encyclopedia of local lore. The tour includes a break for brunch at Caffe Luna Piena (*see* Eats, *below*).

The Mission

The Mission District due east of the Castro derives its name from the **Mission Dolores** (✉ Dolores and 16th Sts., ☎ 415/621–8203), which has stood here since 1791. During the 19th century the Mission was San Francisco's resort community. It gradually changed into a working-class residential neighborhood, and then a largely Latino one, which it remains today. Over the past couple of decades many lesbians and Asian families have begun moving here as well.

The major commercial blocks are **16th Street** from about Guerrero Street to Mission Street, and **Mission and Valencia streets** from 16th Street to 24th Street. You'll find cheap and tasty ethnic cuisine (from Salvadoran to Lebanese), left-leaning and lesbian-oriented shops and galleries, and some of the city's queer and women's performance spaces mixed in among the many Latin American and Chinese groceries and dry-goods stores. The neighborhood, with its low, quirky skyline, is more aesthetically varied and less predictable than the Castro.

Wandering the Mission, you'll discover great places to buy books on feminist issues, New Age themes, and Eastern religion (*see* Gay Media *in* The Little Black Book, *below*). The area is also home to **Community Thrift** (⊠ 623 Valencia St., ☎ 415/861–4910), where the sales of secondhand clothing, shoes, furniture, and household items benefit local queer charities; **Groger's Western Wear** (⊠ 1445 Valencia St., ☎ 415/647–0700), a good place to find the right gear for two-stepping; **Botanica Yoruba** (⊠ 998 Valencia St., ☎ 415/826–4967), which stocks incense, candles, and oils; and **Good Vibrations** (⊠ 1009 Valencia St., ☎ 415/974–8980), an attractive woman-owned emporium that may be the loveliest erotica boutique you'll ever encounter.

Theater Rhinoceros (⊠ 2926 16th St., ☎ 415/861–5079) is the area's long-standing queer performance space; it always has plays and art pieces going on.

A striking mural illustrating the lives of prominent women over the centuries covers two sides of the **Women's Building** (⊠ 3543 18th St., ☎ 415/431–1180). This community center hosts events, readings, meetings, and workshops for women. Many feminist and lesbian political and social organizations meet at this terrific resource.

If you continue east on 18th Street, you'll reach expansive **Dolores Park,** a gay and lesbian "beach" during the day (the fog rarely affects this neighborhood) that can get dicey at night. East of Mission Street and south of Army Street, the modest residential neighborhood of **Bernal Heights** supposedly has the highest concentration of lesbian-owned houses in the city. There's little of interest for the visitor, though you'll surely come across some of the lesbian landed gentry on Cortland Street, the main commercial strip. Gay supervisor Tom Ammiano lives in Bernal Heights, and this is where kidnapped heiress Patty Hearst was finally rescued from the Symbionese Liberation Army.

Gayification is rapidly spreading into the once-faltering **Potrero Hill** district, which is just east of the Mission and shares that neighborhood's fogless climate. Fun shops and a few good restaurants have opened here, mostly along **18th Street.** Artists and young professionals have snapped up newly constructed lofts and apartments on the north slope of Potrero Hill.

Noe Valley

Some lesbians in the Mission and Bernal Heights aspire to live in more fashionable Noe Valley, with its mixed population of straight yuppies, male couples, and gay women with kids. This quiet neighborhood lies south of the Castro and southwest of the Mission. On any morning you'll find **Chloe's** (⊠ 1399 Church St., ☎ 415/648–4116), a casual diner, packed with locals. The commercial strip, **24th Street** between Church and Diamond streets, has several restaurants and bakeries, a well-stocked organic-foods store, a half-dozen coffeehouses, and some shops and galleries. It's a cruisy scene (for gals and guys) but in a folksy way.

To the west and high above Noe Valley and the Castro is **Twin Peaks,** a double-hump mountain with sweeping views of the entire city. You can drive up here via Twin Peaks Boulevard, or, from Castro and Market streets, take Muni Bus 37.

SoMa

The artsy **SoMa** district resembles New York City's SoHo district in more ways than one. Here, light industry has been replaced by designer studios and nonprofit galleries. A few artists' lofts remain, though as in SoHo, most of the artists have been priced out of the market. The area is also a major enclave of factory-outlet stores. Literally south (well, southeast) of Market Street, SoMa is bounded by the Embarcadero to the northeast, Berry Street to the southeast, and the Central Freeway to the southwest.

Moscone Convention Center and a couple of large hotels attract immediate attention, but the SoMa showstopper is the **San Francisco Museum of Modern Art** (⊠ 151 3rd St., ☎ 415/357–4000), which opened in 1995. Architect Mario Botta designed this striking building, which has a brick facade and a central atrium tower made of alternating bands of black and white stone. Some critics have offered backhanded praise, suggesting that the architecture overshadows the art, but SFMOMA's permanent collection includes pivotal works by Picasso, Matisse, O'Keeffe, Kahlo, Pollock, Warhol, and Diebenkorn; the museum's holdings in photography and multimedia work are also significant.

Across the street from SFMOMA in the block surrounded by 3rd, 4th, Mission, and Howard streets is **Yerba Buena Gardens,** a broad grassy plot with sculpture (including a waterfall tribute to Martin Luther King, Jr.) and promenades. Also here is the **Center for the Arts** (⌧ 701 Mission St., ☎ 415/978–2787), one of the city's most exciting visual and performing-arts spaces. SFMOMA's relocation south of Market (it formerly occupied two floors of the Veterans Building in the Civic Center) has drawn many other cultural organizations to SoMa. The **Ansel Adams Center for Photography** (⌧ 250 4th St., ☎ 415/495–7000) exhibits contemporary and historic photography, some of the latter by Adams himself. The **Cartoon Art Museum** (⌧ 814 Mission St., ☎ 415/546–3922) contains 11,000 pieces tracing the history of animation. The **California Historical Society** (⌧ 678 Mission St., ☎ 415/357–1848) tends to a half-million photographs, 150,000 manuscripts, and countless paintings, books, periodicals, and documents. Within the next few years, the **Mexican Museum** hopes to move here from Fort Mason. The **Jewish Museum** (⌧ 121 Steuart St., ☎ 415/543–8880), already south of Market near the Embarcadero, also plans a move closer to SFMOMA.

On the other side of the highway overpass that feeds onto the Bay Bridge, SoMa takes on a more diverse, underground edge. Below Bryant Street between 2nd and 3rd streets is **South Park,** a shaded oasis with picnic tables, a children's playground, and a regular weekday crowd of art, computer, and music employees—hence the neighborhood's nickname, Multimedia Gulch. You can grab a cappuccino or have a weekday lunch at the **South Park Cafe** (*see* Eats, *below*).

At night SoMa comes alive as San Francisco's major club campus, for gays and straights alike. Gay leather and bear bars have been centered here for years, mostly around 8th and 11th streets. Some of the wilder ones (the Black and Blue, the Ambush, and the Boot Camp) closed in the wake of AIDS, but the S.F. Eagle and a few others remain. Several big discos pulse with activity around Folsom and Harrison streets. The area has a few great leather shops as well. **Stormy Leather** (✉ 1158 Howard St., ☎ 415/626–1672) is dyke-owned and has fetish wear, toys, harnesses, and other leather gear for women; the **Bear Shop** (✉ 367 9th St., ☎ 415/552–1506) sells toys, videos, and magazines for "bears"; and **A Taste of Leather** (✉ 317-A 10th St., ☎ 415/252–9166) is one of the largest leather boutiques on the West Coast.

Downtown

The dense triangle of urbanity east of Van Ness Avenue, north of Market Street, and fringed by the Embarcadero serves as San Francisco's commercial center. Most of the city's hotels and high-end department stores (Neiman-Marcus, Saks, Gump's, Nordstrom) are near or on **Union Square.** The section of **Geary Street** just west of the square constitutes the city's modest Theater Row. **Maiden Lane,** east of the square, holds many high-end boutiques; before the 1906 earthquake it was another of San Francisco's red-light districts. Frank Lloyd Wright designed the **Circle Gallery** (✉ 140 Maiden La., ☎ 415/989–2100), the local Erté representative. The gallery is said to have been the prototype for Wright's Guggenheim Museum design—both have a multi-level circular ramp that winds through the exhibition space.

Northeast of Union Square is the **Financial District,** whose spine, **Montgomery Street,** is often called the "Wall Street of the West." For more than a century following the gold rush of 1849 San Francisco was the financial capital of the western United States; it has been ceding ground to Los Angeles only in recent decades. You'll find the city's tallest skyscrapers in the Financial District. Most notable are the 52-story, granite-and-marble **Bank of America** (✉ Pine and Kearny Sts.), which has a top-floor lounge and restaurant, the Carnelian Room (☎ 415/433–7500), and the 853-foot **Transamerica Pyramid** (✉ 600 Montgomery St.).

The famed **Black Cat** nightclub once thrived at nearby 710 Montgomery Street, drawing gays and bohemian types. Early gay activist-entertainer José Sarria often ended the night's social proceedings with a solidarity-enhancing chorus of "God Save Us Nellie Queens." The always outrageous Sarria later became the first openly gay person in the nation to run for public office when he campaigned for a seat on the San Francisco Board of Supervisors in 1961. He lost, but his 5,600 votes helped motivate future queer political activities.

East of the Financial District is the **Embarcadero,** a surface roadway that wraps around the waterfront from Fisherman's Wharf south beyond the San Francisco–Oakland Bay Bridge. Focal points are the **Ferry Building,** erected in 1896 (its distinctive 230-foot clock tower has appeared in countless photos, films, and TV shows), and the mammoth **Embarcadero Center,** which houses offices, shops, a five-screen art cinema, and the Hyatt Regency hotel. Between the Hyatt and the Ferry Building is **Justin Herman Plaza,** a brick-and-concrete park where corporate types spend recess chatting over sandwiches.

There's not a lot to do along the Embarcadero beyond taking a stroll to admire the views of Treasure Island, the Bay Bridge, and the East Bay. Old-fashioned lamps line the Embarcadero's median strip, and the buildings on the various piers have gracefully arched facades. When it's finished, the concrete-and-glass **Promenade Ribbon,** embedded in the sidewalk along the Embarcadero's bay side, will become—or so says the city's Art Commission—America's longest work of art, stretching from Telegraph Hill to South Beach.

The Embarcadero below Market Street is in various stages of rejuvenation. Under the Bay Bridge around Brannan Street is Bayview Village, a development of contemporary condos with shops and restaurants tucked beneath them. Nearby South Beach Marina holds more of the same. This area is only gentrified the first few blocks in from the Embarcadero, meaning that residents here are cut off from much of the city, though they do brush up against SoMa's restaurant, arts, and club scene.

If you head west of the Financial District, you'll approach **Chinatown,** which, for full effect, you should enter via the ornate **Chinatown Gate** at Grant Avenue and Bush Street. This is one of the largest Chinese communities in North America. You're now on the eastern slope of **Nob Hill,** where the city's old money has traditionally come to nest. At the peak of the hill, where California and Mason streets intersect, sit five of the city's most luxurious hotels (the Fairmont, Mark Hopkins, and Huntington among them) and **Grace Cathedral** (⌧ 1051 Taylor St.). The congregation's AIDS Memorial Chapel contains a sculpture by the late Keith Haring and always has panels from the AIDS Memorial Quilt on exhibit. If it's cocktail hour, visit the Fairmont Hotel's tacky, touristy, tropical (complete with rain forest) **Tonga Room** (⊠ 950 Mason St., ☎ 415/772–5000). The Mark Hopkins Inter-Continental is famous for the **Top of the Mark** (⊠ California and Mason Sts., ☎ 415/392–3434), a skyline cocktail bar with expansive plate-glass windows that provide a panoramic view of San Francisco in all directions. The Top of the Mark developed a reputation as a discreet hub of gay social activity throughout the '40s—a place where queer military types could mingle without fear of the vice raids that plagued gay establishments around town. The bar has lost some of its luster these days, but you can't beat the view.

California Street has one of the city's cable-car routes. To find out how the cars work, stop by the free **Cable Car Museum** (⊠ 1201 Mason St., ☎ 415/474–1887).

Just northwest of Nob Hill lies **Russian Hill,** with restored Victorians, fancy new high-rises, and the oft-photographed **Lombard Street** (a.k.a. the crookedest street in the world), which switchbacks eight times from its apex at Hyde Street to its base at Leavenworth Street.

North of Nob Hill and Chinatown is the half-yuppie and half-Italian neighborhood of **North Beach,** whose **Columbus Avenue** and **Stockton Street** overflow with pastry shops and boutiques. The now largely straight and touristy drag bar **Finocchio's** opened officially in 1933 (it had been an illicit speakeasy for several years prior) on Sutter Street before moving to its current location at 506 Broadway. For a time both locations drew a significantly faggy crowd. In the late 1930s lesbians began hanging out in a basement bar called Mona's at 140 Columbus Avenue. Co-owner Mona Sargent didn't realize at first that some of her boyish-looking patrons were actually women, but she took the news in stride and eventually became something of a den mother to the clientele.

Gay writers Allen Ginsberg and Gregory Corso were among the Beat Generation artistes who began hanging around North Beach cafés and clubs in the 1950s. (Jack Kerouac put on a macho show, but if you believe Gore Vidal's memoir *Palimpsest,* Jack walked on the wild side, too, as did, most certainly, his muse Neal Cassady.) The Beats' memory lives on at the **City Lights Bookstore** (⊠ 261 Columbus

Ave., ☎ 415/362–8193), still the domain of poet Lawrence Ferlinghetti.

If the crowds along Columbus Avenue become overwhelming, take a stroll up **Grant Avenue,** a modest commercial and residential strip with an authentically Italian-American ambience. You'll find several purveyors of pastries, cheeses, and sausages, plus some curio shops and used- and designer-clothing stores. When Grant hits Filbert Street, walk east to reach **Telegraph Hill** and the steps to 180-foot **Coit Tower,** which yields fine views of San Francisco Bay and Alcatraz Island.

Polk Gulch and the Tenderloin

Here's a favorite San Francisco joke: "Whaddya do if you find a quarter lying on Polk Street? Kick it over to Van Ness and pick it up." **Polk Street** defines "rough trade" and the phrase, "Brother can you spare a dime?" Hustlers sit along the curb bumming smokes off passersby. Drunken old men stumble out of some of the city's dreariest gay bars and porn shops at two in the afternoon (and two in the morning). Though Polk Street is actually fashionable up around Russian Hill, the section that runs through the heart of the **Polk Gulch** neighborhood, from about Pine Street to McAllister, is on the ratty side.

From the end of World War II, when San Francisco's gay community first began to emerge in strong numbers, until the early '70s, when the action shifted into the Castro, Polk Gulch was the city's most significant gay district. It looks better today than it did five years ago, as certain blocks are slowly being gentrified.

East from lower Polk Street, Eddy and Turk streets lead into the infamous **Tenderloin,** home to many gay and straight strip joints and porn emporiums. This area had a strong gay presence even before Polk Street, though most of the folks who remember these days tend to mutter to themselves in the few remaining, mostly empty gay bars here. Gay hangouts in the Tenderloin were frequent sites of police harassment and raids throughout the middle part of this century, when transgenders and gay males, many of them prostitutes, were regularly rounded up and sometimes physically abused.

Fisherman's Wharf and the Marina District

San Francisco's northern waterfront, from North Beach to the Golden Gate Bridge, contains many touristy attractions.

Along much-publicized **Fisherman's Wharf** are several formerly industrial blocks and piers with amusements, schlocky shops, and overpriced restaurants. The action stretches from **Ghirardelli Square,** at the top of Polk Street, to **Pier 39,** home to the tackiest of souvenir stands and the recently opened **Underwater World** (☎ 415/544–9920), an aquarium overflowing with native marine life.

From several piers here you can book sightseeing cruises of the bay or excursions to **Alcatraz Island** (☎ 415/546–2628), the infamous prison. Tours of Alcatraz are a must-do—the audio narration by former prisoners and guards is worth the extra fee. The 15-minute boat ride to the island affords great views of the city's skyline. Once there, U.S. Park Service rangers offer tours on everything from the island's ecology to its military history.

Just west of all of this action is the impressive **National Maritime Museum** (⊠ Polk St., at Beach St., ☎ 415/556–3002), and beyond that lies **Fort Mason** (☎ 415/979–3010 for events information), a former World War II supply depot that now contains several cultural attractions, including the **Mexican Museum** (⊠ Bldg. D, ☎ 415/441–0404), the **Museo Italo-Americano** (⊠ Bldg. C, ☎ 415/673–2200), the **San Francisco African-American Historical and Cultural Society** (⊠ Bldg. C, ☎ 415/441–0640), and the **San Francisco Craft and Folk Art Museum** (⊠ Bldg. A, ☎ 415/775–0990). The **Magic Theatre** (⊠ Bldg. D, ☎ 415/441–8822) is one of several theater groups headquartered here.

Farther west is the **Marina district,** a monied neighborhood where yuppies and executives nest in art deco apartments and Spanish-style homes. The only significant site here is the **Palace of Fine Arts** (⊠ Baker St. at Beach St.), a massive study in rococo grandeur erected for the 1915 Panama-Pacific International Exposition and restored in the 1960s. Its interior houses the **Exploratorium** (☎ 415/561–0362), a science museum that resembles a crowded airport hangar. Displays are hands-on. Touch this, listen to that, open these, put your finger under this, rest your chin over here—it's like playing Twister with 700 strangers.

West of here is the 1,400-acre **Presidio,** now administered as part of the Golden Gate National Recreation Area. From the time that Spanish settlers first claimed the area in 1776 until the U.S. Army relinquished control in 1994, the Presidio was a military post. At the northwest tip of the Presidio, the awesome **Golden Gate Bridge** stretches her arms across the bay, connecting San Francisco with the Marin Headlands.

Abutting the Presidio is **Baker Beach**; its southwesternmost end is sandy and easily accessible. As you hike along the rocky coastline in a northeasterly direction, toward the Golden Gate Bridge, you'll discover that much of the crowd is sunbathing in the nude (weather permitting), that some of these sunbathers are gay men, and that many of them are a bit frisky. Always watch your footing along the steep trails and slippery rocks—and again, beware of the dangerous surf.

Southwest of the Presidio is rugged 275-acre **Lincoln Park.** The park's sheer cliffs provide views of the Pacific Ocean, often accompanied by high winds, dense fog, and pounding surf. One of the better vantage points is **Land's End** (parking is at the end of El Camino del Mar). If you've read Armistead Maupin's *Tales of the City,* you'll remember this perch as being fraught with danger (the cliff here is very steep). The beach down below is quite cruisy. Be careful, though—the Park Service administers this stretch, so any misdeed here is literally a federal offense. Swimming at any of the beaches off Lincoln Park is not recommended, as there's a strong and violent undertow.

If you're in need of a cultural fix while in Lincoln Park, drop into the refurbished **California Palace of the Legion of Honor** (⊠ 34th Ave., off Clement St., ☎ 415/863–3330). The galleries on the Legion's upper level contain European art spanning the past seven centuries; on the lower level is a mix of prints and drawings, European porcelain, and ancient art. South of Lincoln Park the **Cliff House** (⊠ 1066 Point Lobos Ave.) is worth seeing if only for the views. The food at its restaurant and the trinkets sold at its gift shop are overpriced and mediocre, though the hefty brunch served in the upstairs eatery isn't bad and the vista is particularly winning on a sunny day. On the lowest level, the Musée Mécanique houses an amusing collection of antique arcade games.

West of Van Ness Avenue

Ritzy **Pacific Heights** is known for its expensive homes, classy shops, and trendy restaurants. This is a fairly straight area, populated mainly by yuppies who work in the Financial District. **Fillmore Street,** which runs north to south, holds dozens of cute shops and cafés. Sunny days bring out bikini-briefed bathers to the southwest slope of **Lafayette Park** (⊠ Sacramento St., at Laguna St.) which occasionally still lives up to its '60s–'70s appellation, the Gay Riviera. Just north of Pacific Heights in Cow Hollow another strip of boutiques and restaurants lines **Union Street** from Steiner Street to Gough (pronounced "Goff") Street.

South of Pacific Heights is **Japantown,** a contemporary and characterless neighborhood where the city's Japanese immigrants settled prior to World War II; during the war most were placed in internment camps. Many Japanese returned after the war. The area's mammoth **Japan Center** (⊠ Post St. between Laguna and Fillmore Sts.) houses shops, restaurants, and a multiplex. To unwind from a long day of touring, have a shiatsu massage or a steam bath at the very fine **Kabuki Hot Springs** (⊠ 1750 Geary Blvd., ☎ 415/922–6000).

Southeast of Japantown, near the intersection of Van Ness and Market, is the **Civic Center,** the city's central complex of municipal buildings and cultural institutions. The dramatic French Renaissance Revival **City Hall** (⊠ Polk and Grove Sts.) is closed for seismic retrofitting until late 1998. The interior of the **San Francisco Public Library** (⊠ Larkin and Grove Sts., ☎ 415/557–4440) is anchored by a sweeping central atrium, off of which are 11 special-interest centers that focus on Asian-Americans, African-Americans, the environment, and lesbians and gays. The state-of-the-art library (it opened in 1996) has 300 computers with free Internet access, along with other technological research tools. The on-site **James C. Hormel Gay and Lesbian Center** (☎ 415/557–4566), the first of its kind, holds books, periodicals, photographs, and other artifacts of gay life. Exhibits and documents trace local history but also provide an excellent overview of queer culture around the world. The room is filled with plush armchairs and writing desks; brushing up on our history has never been such a treat.

San Francisco's world-class ballet and opera companies usually perform at the **War Memorial Opera House** (⊠ 301 Van Ness Ave., ☎ 415/861–4008). The 1932 building should reopen for the opera's fall 1997 season following a 21-month seismic retrofit. Disco diva and local legend Sylvester rocked the joint with a memorable performance in 1979. A block away is the newer **Louise M. Davies Symphony Hall** (⊠ 201

Van Ness Ave., ☎ 415/552–8000). Gay conductor Michael Tilson Thomas leads the band (the San Francisco Symphony). The nearby **San Francisco Performing Arts Library and Museum** (✉ 399 Grove St., ☎ 415/255–4800) contains a large collection of memorabilia of the city's illustrious performing-arts history.

One constructive by-product of San Francisco's 1989 earthquake was the destruction of a Central Freeway ramp that passed over the **Western Addition,** just west of the Civic Center. The eastern part of this neighborhood, whose commercial heart runs along **Hayes Street,** from Van Ness Avenue to Laguna Street, is known as **Hayes Valley.** Gentrification of this underappreciated district began as soon as the freeway ramp tumbled. Galleries and funky restaurants now line Hayes Street and the blocks just off it.

Just west of here is **Alamo Square,** bordered by Scott, Hayes, Steiner, and Fulton streets. The hilly green slope, best approached via Fulton Street, is surrounded by many of the city's restored "painted ladies," those colorful Victorian row houses coated with as many as two dozen shades of paint.

The Haight

Haight Street slices through the heart of the **Haight-Ashbury** district, one of the world's most recognizable beds of counterculturalism. The area's history is typical of other hippie neighborhoods around the country. It has some of the city's biggest and most desirable homes, in this case Victorian and Edwardian wood-frame affairs. During the '50s and early '60s, when the middle class headed for the suburbs, young artists and radical thinkers began taking over, converting the oversize homes into communes or chopping them up into affordable apartments. Progressive rockers such as the Grateful Dead, Janis Joplin, and the Jefferson Airplane lived here, as did their thousands of acid-infused followers.

This part of town remains a land of slackers and alternateens, an easy place to find crystal jewelry, incense, vintage duds, and illicit buds. It has changed some with the times, however: Deadheads are outnumbered by grungers, and rave-wear is more prevalent than tie-dyes (though just barely on Haight Street itself). Most of the excessively commercial shops are in the Upper Haight, from about Masonic Avenue to Schrader Street.

The Lower Haight, east of Divisadero and technically outside the Haight–Ashbury proper, resembles the old Haight more than the actual one. The Lower Haight has an authentic struggling-artist mood—it's a good spot to find cheap food and poor students nagging you for spare change.

Beautiful **Buena Vista Park** rises high above the center of the Haight, allowing fabulous views in all directions. This is the city's cruisiest park—no matter what time of day. It's a tad dangerous; in 1996, for example, the park was plagued by a seductive pickpocket. He was eventually apprehended, but such behavior is not uncommon here. The police drop by frequently and usually show no mercy, though a few years back they reportedly cut a high-profile local pro football player some slack after they caught him out on a midnight troll.

Golden Gate Park

Golden Gate Park lies between Fulton Street and Lincoln Way, and stretches all the way from Stanyan Street to the Pacific Ocean. Meadows, groves of cypress trees, lakes, and trails meander through the park, a wonderful spot for biking or blading—especially on Sundays when most of its roads are closed to vehicles. The eastern half has several notable attractions, such as the **Strybing Arboretum** (☎ 415/661–1316), the **Asian Art Museum** (☎ 415/668–8921), the **de Young Museum** (☎ 415/863–3330), and the **California Academy of Sciences** (☎ 415/750–7145). The academy contains a planetarium, an aquarium, an "earthquake floor" enabling visitors to experience a simulated quake, and several art and natural-history exhibits.

The Willis Polk–designed **Beach Chalet** at the west end of the park was built in 1925, but had been closed for two decades until a restoration project was completed in early 1997. The walls of a ground-level visitor center are covered by Lucien Labaudt's WPA-era mural depicting San Francisco life earlier in this century. A three-dimensional model in the center shows just how grand, in several respects, Golden Gate Park is. Upstairs there's a brew-pub restaurant with views of **Ocean Beach** and (on sunny days) beyond. The chalet's reopening and a concurrent underbrush-clearing project have considerably reduced the action at a formerly hopping cruising area on the paths between two nearby windmills. The **Queen Wilhelmina Tulip Garden** is below the working windmill.

GETTING AROUND

Up until a few years ago, San Francisco was an easy driving city. It's still not too hard to find parking spaces west of Van Ness Avenue, but downtown as well as points north and south are getting tougher, and parking in most residential areas (including the Castro) for more than two hours requires a permit. Garages downtown are costly, too—the best (and cheapest) bets are the Sutter-Stockton and the 5th and Mission. This city has steep streets, which can prove tricky if you're driving a stick shift. The main reason to have a car here is to explore the outlying areas; in the city itself, unless you're dead-set on being able to drive around at will, you should consider relying on mass transit and cabs.

Muni (☎ 415/673–6864) buses are a good way to see the city. From anywhere on Market Street you can pick up Muni Bus 8 to reach the Castro—or try one of the antique F-line trolleys, including an open-air number from Blackpool. The fare is $1, exact change (bills or coins) is required; day passes are available. Muni light-rail cars also stop at Castro and Market.

Cable cars ($2) are fun and exciting, but they only hit a few major sights. **BART** (☎ 415/992–2278) trains (fare varies) are useful for getting to Berkeley and Oakland, but are less practical for travel within San Francisco. Still, many people use BART to commute between downtown and the Mission. Taxis are difficult to hail but can be phoned—**Yellow Cab** (☎ 415/626–2345) is one option—or picked up at most hotels. San Francisco is a small city, so even a ride from downtown to the Castro shouldn't set you back more than $8. In SoMa, taxis are usually plentiful after the clubs close; in the Castro, you can sometimes hail a cab at Castro and Market streets.

Taking a cab from San Francisco's airport (SFO) into town costs about $30. **Super Shuttle** (☎ 415/558–8500) vans stop at upper-level traffic islands at each of the terminals (signs are posted). The shuttles will take you anywhere in the city for $12 ($8 for the second passenger to the same destination). Pick up the **SFO Airporter** (☎ 415/495–8404) bus ($9) outside the baggage claim area for service to downtown hotels.

City Transport

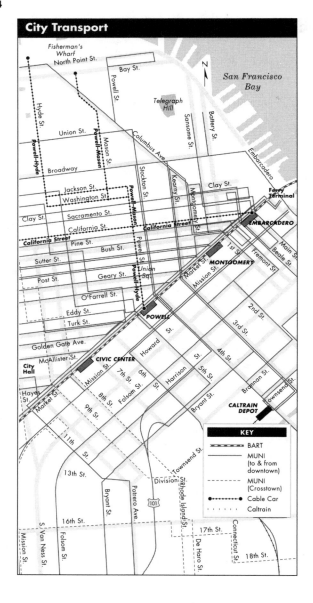

Fisherman's Wharf
North Point St.
Bay St.
Powell St.
San Francisco Bay
Telegraph Hill
Hyde St.
Powell-Hyde
Union St.
Powell-Mason
Mason St.
Columbus Ave.
Sansome St.
Battery St.
Embarcadero
Broadway
Jackson St.
Washington St.
Stockton St.
Powell-Mason
Kearny St.
Montgomery St.
Clay St.
Ferry Terminal
Clay St.
Sacramento St.
California St.
California Street
California Street
EMBARCADERO
Main St.
Pine St.
Powell St.
Bush St.
Montgomery St.
1st St.
Fremont St.
Beale St.
MONTGOMERY
Sutter St.
Powell-Hyde
Union Sq.
Post St.
Geary St.
Market St.
Mission St.
O'Farrell St.
Eddy St.
Turk St.
POWELL
2nd St.
3rd St.
Golden Gate Ave.
Howard St.
McAllister St.
CIVIC CENTER
4th St.
City Hall
Mission St.
7th St.
6th St.
Harrison St.
5th St.
Brannan St.
Hayes St.
Market St.
8th St.
Folsom St.
St.
Bryant St.
CALTRAIN DEPOT
Townsend St.
9th St.
11th St.
13th St.
Townsend St.
Division St.
Rhode Island St.
101
Bryant St.
Potrero Ave.
16th St.
17th St.
De Haro St.
Connecticut St.
S. Van Ness St.
Mission St.
Folsom St.
18th St.

KEY

- ▬▬▬ BART
- ——— MUNI (to & from downtown)
- – – – MUNI (Crosstown)
- •••••• Cable Car
- ⋯⋯⋯ Caltrain

WHEN TO GO

There is no bad time to visit San Francisco, although summer tends to have the highest incidence of fog and damp weather. Fall and spring are both consistently crowded and delightful. Winter, sometimes overlooked, can be sunny and beautiful when most of the country is suffering through snow or rain. All year the temperature in the city rarely zips above the 80s, though it can get nippy at night.

San Francisco's drag extravaganza **Wigstock West** (☎ 415/273–5979) kicks up its heels every May. The **San Francisco Lesbian, Gay, Bisexual, Transgender Pride Celebration** (☎ 415/864–3733) is usually the last week in June, sometimes the third. The event draws well over a quarter-million people. Two major fall events are the always-wild **Folsom Street Fair** (☎ 415/861–3257) on the last Sunday in September, and the **Castro Street Fair** (☎ 415/467–3354) on the first weekend in October. San Francisco's wildly campy **Halloween celebration** (☎ 415/777–5500) took place in the Castro for many years but moved to the Civic Center in 1996 to accommodate the incredible crowds. It's still plenty of fun.

The **San Francisco International Lesbian and Gay Film Festival** drew more than 50,000 visitors in 1996—it's been getting stronger every year since its inception in 1977, when a few local filmmakers presented their own Super-8 productions in the old gay community center on Page Street. In terms of prestige and the number of Hollywood producers it draws, the event is beginning to become the gay version of Robert Redford's Sundance Festival. It's held for 10 days in late June, coinciding with gay pride.

EATS

San Francisco may be America's best dining city—it is very difficult to stumble upon a bad meal. At worst, you'll pay too much in touristy areas, and the food will be decent but not great. Or in less-expensive neighborhoods, you might sample a mediocre meal, but your financial loss will be minimal. In any case, disappointments are rare.

What follows are some broad guidelines to consider when exploring various neighborhoods:

Downtown and the Financial District: Pricey, but usually ambitious well-prepared cuisine. **Chinatown:** Maybe the best one in America (although some of the city's top purveyors of Chinese cuisine are elsewhere); if you have to ask for chopsticks, move on. **North Beach:** Delicious moderately priced Italian food—all styles, including one that is purely North Beach. **Fisherman's Wharf:** Don't eat here. **Pacific Heights:** Many darlings of regional Cal cuisine—healthy, light, but pricey; lots of interesting wine lists. **Marina:** Singles-oriented neighborhood restaurants where straight yuppies let their hair down. **Japantown:** self-explanatory. **Hayes Valley and the Civic Center:** Many up-and-coming bistros; a place to nosh and be noticed. **The Haight:** Sullen young misfits snarfing down cheap comfort food. **Richmond and Sunset:** No glitter here, but some surprisingly good neighborhood spots—ask locals for favorites. **SoMa:** You just never know . . . some of San Francisco's hottest restaurants rub shoulders with some of its coldest cafeterias. **The Mission:** Cheap, delicious, healthy fare—Formica tables, burritos, tofu. **Noe Valley:** Breakfast is serious business here, and there are several upbeat coffeehouses, too. **The Castro:** Lots of local color and some hot new restaurants, but be careful at the low end—the greasy spoons in particular can be lousy.

For price ranges, *see* the dining chart at the front of this guide.

The Castro

$$–$$$ ✕ **Mecca.** Many consider this supper club the true star of Market Street, and the long lines outside seem to support the claim. Mecca's patrons come to enjoy the stylish decor and chef Lynn Sheehan's Mediterranean-inspired cuisine—semolina gnocchi, spiced rack of lamb with a roast-tomato and cracked-grain salad, and sautéed halibut on a celeriac potato puree. ⊠ *2029 Market St.,* ☎ *415/621–7000.*

$$–$$$ ✕ **2223.** This hopping gay restaurant (formerly known as "No Name" or "Market Street Restaurant") is alive with gossip, cruising, and fun, and the air is filled with the aroma of outstanding California cuisine. Roasted monkfish, portobello mushroom soup, and braised lentils and broccoli rabe with roasted-red-pepper rouille are among the highlights. On weekends, the brunches pull in everyone who's anyone. ⊠ *2223 Market St.,* ☎ *415/431–0692.*

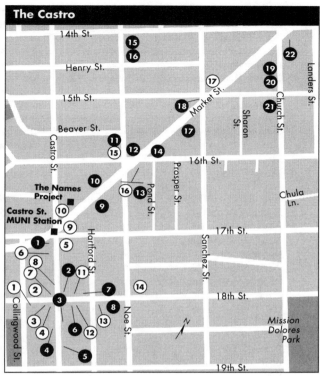

The Castro

Eats ●

Anchor Oyster Bar, **5**
Bad Man Jose's, **6**
Bagdad Café, **14**
Cafe Flore, **12**
Caffe Luna Piena, **4**
Castro Country Club, **7**
Hot'n'Hunky, **8**
Josie's Cabaret and Juice Joint, **13**

Jumpin' Java, **15**
Just Desserts, **20**
La Méditerranée, **11**
Marcello's, **1**
Mecca, **22**
No-Name Sushi, **21**
Pasqua, **2**
Pasta Pomodoro, **10**
Patio Café, **3**
Pozole, **9**

Sparky's, **19**
Take Sushi, **16**
Thai House, **18**
2223, **17**

Scenes ○

Badlands, **3**
The Cafe, **9**
Cafe du Nord, **17**
Castro Station, **8**
Daddy's, **6**
Detour, **10**

Edge, **1**
Harvey's, **4**
Josie's Cabaret and Juice Joint, **16**
Men's Room, **14**
Metro, **15**
Midnight Sun, **12**
Moby Dick, **13**
Pendulum, **2**
Phoenix, **7**
Twin Peaks, **5**
Uncle Bert's, **11**

$$ \quad ✕ **Anchor Oyster Bar.** Meal for meal, this upbeat restaurant is one of the Castro's most dependable haunts. You'll never be treated to less than wonderful clam chowder or any of a number of fresh pastas and seafood grills. Cheerful, if slow, staff. ⊠ *579 Castro St.,* ☎ *415/431–3990.*

$$ \quad ✕ **Caffe Luna Piena.** Trevor Hailey, famous for her queer walking tours of the Castro, brings her flock to this hot Castro restaurant for brunch as part of the trip. With dining in a lush garden and excellent regional cooking either for brunch or dinner (consider sesame-crusted catfish and oatmeal-almond French toast), Luna Piena is like the nearby Patio Café updated for the '90s. ⊠ *558 Castro St.,* ☎ *415/621–2566.*

$–$$ \quad ✕ **La Méditerranée.** This Middle Eastern and Greek eatery serves some of the best under-$10 dinners in the city. You'll find all the usual Greek dishes, plus Lebanese kibbeh (ground lamb) and tangy *baba ganoush* (eggplant puree with lemon juice, olive oil, tahini, and garlic). The combo platters are hearty and inexpensive, and you can get picnic meals to take to Buena Vista Park. ⊠ *288 Noe St.,* ☎ *415/431–7210.*

$–$$ \quad ✕ **No-Name Sushi.** Credited with offering the Castro's best sushi bang for your buck, the No-Name (also known as but rarely called "Nippon Sushi") often has long lines, especially on weekends. It's worth any inconvenience, however. The fish is fresh and expertly prepared. ⊠ *314 Church St., no phone. No credit cards.*

$–$$ \quad ✕ **Pasta Pomodoro.** There's nothing fancy or particularly memorable about this cheerful pasta joint on Market, except that scads of queens dine here night after night. The owners must be doing something right. ⊠ *2304 Market St.,* ☎ *415/ 558–8123.*

$–$$ \quad ✕ **Patio Café.** Not surprisingly, a pretty garden patio (with faux tropical birds) provides the setting. This just may be the queerest patio in America: Sunday brunches are usually mobbed with hungover disco queens dishing the previous night's tricks and treats. The food is just so-so. ⊠ *531 Castro St.,* ☎ *415/621–4640.*

$–$$ \quad ✕ **Pozole.** At this lively spot along Market Street, many admire the trompe l'oeil decor and the gorgeous wait staff (few of whom speak any English), known affectionately as the "boys of Pozole" (they're so cute, several have agents). Often overlooked is the cheap and extraordinarily good Mexican food, which emphasizes enchiladas and quesadillas with a mix of traditional and innovative ingredients. The burrito

Maya (sautéed pork with a smoked-sweet-chili, cinnamon, roasted-tomato, orange, and tequila sauce) is a standout. The chipotle salsa is delicious. ⊠ *2337 Market St.,* ☎ *415/626–2666. No credit cards.*

$–$$ ✕ **Thai House.** Several good Thai restaurants can be found in the Castro, yet no one seems to agree on which one is best. Here's a vote for one of the gayest, whose specialties include pungent green curries. Be sure to sample the sweet-and-smoky Thai iced coffee. ⊠ *2200 Market St.,* ☎ *415/864–5006.*

$ ✕ **Bad Man José's.** This taqueria has an Aztec-influenced decor that's straight out of an archaeological dig—right down to the huge earthen likenesses of Aztec gods lining the walls. Try the Tiburón tacos—two broiled thresher-shark tacos made with soft-corn tortillas, cabbage, tartar sauce, and poblano hot sauce. The veggie tacos are great, too. ⊠ *4077 18th St.,* ☎ *415/861–1706. No credit cards.*

$ ✕ **Bagdad Café.** Some people call it "the Fag Hag Café," but the crowd—and especially the staff—is lesbo-chic. The food at this 24-hour diner is better and healthier than Sparky's, the Castro's other post-disco nosh pit. But that isn't saying much. ⊠ *2295 Market St.,* ☎ *415/621–4434. No credit cards.*

$ ✕ **Hot 'n' Hunky.** Many people swear by the juicy burgers here; though they're good and have amusing names (e.g., "I wanna hold your ham") they're hardly the stuff of legend. Obviously, the name of the place suggests that you turn your eyes toward the waiters, and they do measure up nicely—not because they're so beefy but rather because they're so fun and dishy. Great jukebox. ⊠ *4039 18th St.,* ☎ *415/621–6365.*

$ ✕ **Josie's Cabaret and Juice Joint.** This crunchy nonalcoholic café serves inexpensive vegetarian food and yummy fruit smoothies during the day; at night it becomes a showcase for queer entertainers (*see* Scenes, *below*). ⊠ *3583 16th St.,* ☎ *415/861–7933.*

$ ✕ **Marcello's.** Across from the Castro Theatre and steps from several bars is a great option for quick pizza—even the ready-made slices include such toppings as ham-and-pineapple. A whole pie can be pricey but will feed an army. ⊠ *420 Castro St.,* ☎ *415/863–3900. No credit cards.*

$ ✕ **Sparky's.** After the Castro bars close a mostly young, vaguely trendy bunch of queens congregates here for filling tuna melts, burgers, fries, and other greasy delights. It's open all night. ⊠ *242 Church St.,* ☎ *415/621–6001. No credit cards.*

$ ✕ **Take Sushi.** Betty, the owner here, is something of a neighborhood mom—she seems to know everyone who drops into her tiny Japanese restaurant. ⊠ *149 Noe St.,* ☎ *415/621–0290. No credit cards.*

Noe Valley, the Mission District, and Potrero Hill

$$$– ✕ **Flying Saucer.** Quirky and loads of fun, this is one of the
$$$$ priciest restaurants in the Mission. Few diners complain, though. They generally leave satisfied by the large, artfully presented portions of California cuisine and wowed by the eye-pleasing decor. ⊠ *1000 Guerrero St.,* ☎ *415/641–9955.*

$$–$$$ ✕ **Firefly.** First dates and long-term lovers will feel equally at home at this understated Noe Valley restaurant, where after a few visits the charming servers know you by name. The oft-changing menu is nowhere near so familiar, with an enticing brand of home-style cooking that incorporates a United Nations of ingredients. Crawfish risotto cakes and barbecued Cornish game hen are two favorites. The desserts alone are worth the trip; check out the banana bread pudding in caramel sauce. ⊠ *4288 24th St.,* ☎ *415/821–7652.*

$$–$$$ ✕ **Timo's.** A yuppified take on a Spanish tapas bar, this purple-and-green always-packed Mission place suffers a bit from slow service. Many dishes are traditional (salt cod, marinated mushrooms), but others—such as cassoulet of duck confit—span the whole of Europe. There's a dance floor in back. ⊠ *842 Valencia St.,* ☎ *415/647–0558.*

$$–$$$ ✕ **Universal Café.** One of the Mission's rising stars has a striking postmodern dining room set inside a converted turn-of-the-century warehouse. Bountiful floral arrangements offset the spare look of metal chairs and marble counters and tabletops. The menu concentrates on French and Italian Mediterranean fare—try the roasted Muscovy duck on spaghetti squash with chanterelle and porcini mushrooms. The grilled flatbread, which comes with an array of toppings, makes a fine starter. ⊠ *2814 19th St.,* ☎ *415/821–4608.*

$$–$$$ ✕ **Val 21.** Named for its location at the corner of Valencia and 21st streets, this purveyor of healthful Cal cuisine changes its menu every six weeks. Featured entrées include fish and free-range poultry dishes, vegetarian plates—such as grilled portobello mushrooms on a soft roasted-red-pepper polenta—and no red meat. Jazz music pumps through the stylish industrial-looking dining room. ⊠ *995 Valencia St.,* ☎ *415/821–6622.*

$$ ✕ Slow Club. One of the many quasi-tapas pads that have become all the rage in San Francisco, and especially in the Mission District, the Slow Club presents a diverse menu of California-inspired small plates. Roasted Yukon potatoes with aioli, and mussels sautéed in a tarragon-saffron cream sauce are among the highlights. The sophisticated postmodern-deco decor encourages a fashionable clientele. ⊠ *2501 Mariposa St.,* ☎ *415/241–9390.*

$–$$ ✕ La Rondalla. It's hard to tell whether the food here is truly extraordinary, or whether it simply seems great because all the authentic Mexican kitsch—bright and colorful lights, Christmas paraphernalia, and stuffed birds—distracts you. The food comes in giant heaps, enough to fill you up before a night of dancing at nearby Esta Noche. If you're lucky, the tuneful mariachi musicians will serenade you. ⊠ *901 Valencia St.,* ☎ *415/647–7474. No credit cards.*

$–$$ ✕ Radio Valencia Cafe. Even for the Mission, this corner storefront is strange. Crudely painted fanciful scenes adorn old spool tables. The linoleum floor is filthy, fabulous Latin music plays in the background, and the service is indifferent at best. The food—focaccia pizzas with pesto and veggies, a

Texas tuna sandwich with apples, kidney beans, and onions—
is good, not great. It's the kind of place that might inspire
you to write a Raymond Carveresque short story. ⊠ *1199
Valencia St.,* ☎ *415/826–1199.*

$–$$ ✕ **Ti-Couz.** Lots of cute dykes work at this delightful creperie
where you can invent your own crepe or choose from a long
list. These Gallic wonders are tasty and reasonably priced.
You might also pop in for one of the sweeter dessert creations.
⊠ *3108 16th St.,* ☎ *415/252–7373.*

$ ✕ **Just For You.** East of the Mission in Potrero Hill, this
major spot for dykes with tykes has mighty-fine breakfast
burritos. ⊠ *1453 18th St.,* ☎ *415/647–3033. No credit
cards.*

$ ✕ **La Cumbre.** Colorful Mexican art on the walls helps
brighten this otherwise drab eatery. The menu includes huge
authentic burritos, rice-and-bean platters, and award-winning *carne asada* (grilled steak). Though locals overrate it,
this is among the best of the Mission's many taquerias. ⊠
515 Valencia St., ☎ *415/863–8205. No credit cards.*

SoMa

$$$ ✕ **Hawthorne Lane.** Bill Clinton ate at this Postrio spin-off
the night it opened—he's one of many celebrities to test the
Mediterranean- and Asian-inspired victuals. Critics com-
plain that the more formal and expensive of the two dining
sections is the least reliable. Better to feast on rich pizzas and
robustly seasoned small plates in the casual dining area in
front. ⊠ *22 Hawthorne St.,* ☎ *415/777–9779.*

$$–$$$ ✕ **Appam.** Although many types of Asian cuisine are gen-
erously represented in San Francisco, there are only a hand-
ful of Indian restaurants. Appam is a warmly lit space with
exquisite California-inspired food. Soft-shell crab poached
with green peppers and coconut milk is one of the less tra-
ditional standouts, but curries and tandoori grills are also avail-
able. The service is emphatically erratic. ⊠ *1261 Folsom St.,*
☎ *415/626–2798.*

$$–$$$ ✕ **Bizou.** This chic SoMa café with glowing yellow-and-or-
ange hues offers stellar French-Italian comfort food, includ-
ing baked tagliolini with lamb sausage and duck-leg confit
with curried lentils. ⊠ *598 4th St.,* ☎ *415/543–2222.*

$$–$$$ ✕ **Boulevard.** One of the most esteemed restaurants to open
in San Francisco this decade is the joint vision of renowned
chef Nancy Oakes and interior designer Pat Kuleto. The

Eats ●

Appam, **12**
Bizou, **10**
Boulevard, **1**
Butterfield's, **7**
Caffé Centro, **3**
Fringale, **9**
Hamburger Mary's, **13**
Hawthorne Lane, **2**
Lulu, **8**
Manora, **14**
Palette Cafe, **6**
Pizza Love, **11**
Ristorante Ecco, **5**
South Park Cafe, **4**
Woodward's Garden, **15**

Scenes ○

Asia, **4**
The Box, **5**
Club DV8, **2**
Club Townsend, **3**
End Up, **1**
Hole in the Wall Saloon, **9**
Julie's Supper Club, **7**
Litter Box, **10**
Lonestar, **14**
Minna, **8**
My Place, **11**
Powerhouse, **13**
Rawhide II, **6**
S.F. Eagle, **17**
Special K, **15**
Stud, **12**
V/SF, **16**

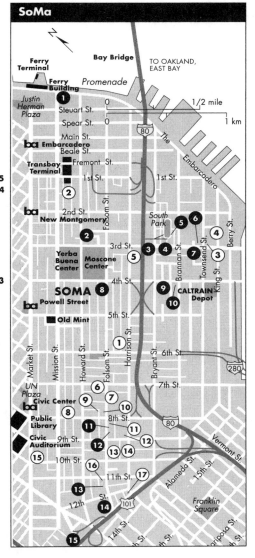

New American menu changes often but is always outstanding; you can dine well for less at the fashionable bar overlooking the exhibition kitchen. ⊠ *1 Mission St.,* ☎ *415/543–6084.*

$$–$$$ ✕ **Fringale.** This French Basque–style restaurant is a real find—a bright café with lemon-yellow walls that feels as if it should be out in the countryside, not on a nasty industrial street. People come from all over town for fare that includes such delicacies as Roquefort ravioli and potato and goat cheese galette. ⊠ *570 4th St.,* ☎ *415/543–0573.*

$$–$$$ ✕ **LuLu.** This chic eating spot is a fabulous renovation of a San Francisco warehouse with a lofty vaulted ceiling; pizzas and pastas with amazing combinations of ingredients keep company on the menu with the signature sizzling mussels roasted in an iron skillet. Less expensive prix-fixe dining is available at the attached LuLu Bis, a family-style space with communal tables. You can nosh on sandwiches and sweets in the LuLu Café. ⊠ *816 Folsom St.,* ☎ *415/495–5775.*

$$–$$$ ✕ **Ristorante Ecco.** The classical decor of this South Park restaurant will transport you right to Tuscany. The extensive antipasto selections are deservedly renowned, and you'll find unusual dishes such as chickpea fritters with an eggplant vinaigrette and a smoked-pheasant salad. ⊠ *101 South Park Ave.,* ☎ *415/495–3291.*

$$–$$$ ✕ **Woodward's Garden.** This nine-table hole-in-the-wall tucked under a freeway was begun by Greens and Postrio alums Margie Conard and Dana Tommasino, who present a limited, thoughtful menu of northern California cuisine. The tight space is romantic in a can't-move-your-elbows sort of way. Conard and Tommasino have one priority: making sure that you leave having eaten one of the best meals of your life. Call well ahead for a table. ⊠ *1700 Mission St.,* ☎ *415/621–7122. No credit cards.*

$$ ✕ **Butterfield's.** Crab salad, griddled rockfish, and fried oysters are some of the mostly New England–style traditional dishes at this excellent and affordable seafood restaurant; there are always several good daily specials, too. It's right around the corner from the nightclub at 177 Townsend. ⊠ *202 Townsend St.,* ☎ *415/281–9001.*

$$ ✕ **Manora.** Fill up on the spicy fish cakes, charbroiled jumbo shrimp, or the garlic quail at this very fine Thai restaurant. ⊠ *1600 Folsom St.,* ☎ *415/861–6224.*

\$\$ ✕ **South Park Cafe.** A long dining room of closely spaced tables, creamy yellow walls, indirect lights, and flowers galore creates an appropriately Parisian mood for delicious bistro fare. Favorites include savory rabbit stew and grilled chicken with pureed roasted-garlic potatoes, wild mushrooms, and thyme sauce. A great spot for breakfast, too. ✉ *108 South Park Ave.,* ☎ *415/495–7275.*

\$ ✕ **Hamburger Mary's.** This major favorite of SoMa disco bunnies is a colorful burger joint (tofu patties are available) that's open till 1 in the morning (2 on weekends). ✉ *1582 Folsom St.,* ☎ *415/626–1985.*

\$ ✕ **Pizza Love.** There's little to love about the mediocre pizza here except that it's available until 4 in the morning on weekends. ✉ *1245 Folsom St.,* ☎ *415/252–5683. No credit cards.*

Civic Center, Hayes Valley, and the Haight

\$\$\$\$ ✕ **Stars.** People take their friends here primarily to impress them, which can be a problem because Stars's holier-than-thou waitrons will blow you off if you're not famous. Nevertheless, this pioneer of California cuisine is justly lauded for its inventive menu, which emphasizes healthful poultry and seafood grills. The casual Stars Cafe, around the corner on Van Ness Avenue, has a limited selection of similar fare at lower prices, though the quality is more variable. ✉ *150 Redwood Alley,* ☎ *415/861–7827.*

\$\$–\$\$\$ ✕ **Carta.** One of the terrific new restaurants leading Market Street's culinary renaissance presents a different culture's cuisine each month. This may sound like a gimmick, but the chefs pull it off with aplomb, serving four weeks of such Venetian favorites as pan-roasted squab with herb-cream polenta and wild mushrooms, then seamlessly switching gears and delivering authentic Thai curries and satays. Oaxacan, Russian, and Moroccan are among the other cuisines that have been featured. ✉ *1772 Market St.,* ☎ *415/863–3516.*

\$\$–\$\$\$ ✕ **Hayes Street Grill.** This informal seafood bistro has a dapper dining room with varnished wood tables and soothing walls of cream and forest green. Some of the better entrées include the crispy soft-shell crab meunière and the grilled fresh calamari. Yuppie central. ✉ *320 Hayes St.,* ☎ *415/863–5545.*

36

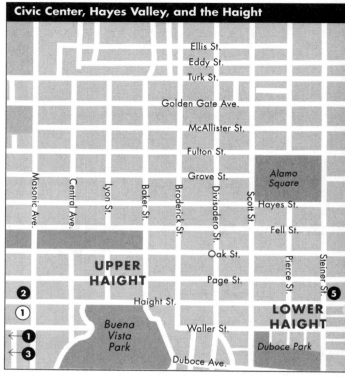

Civic Center, Hayes Valley, and the Haight

Eats ●

Cafe Della Stelle, **15**
Carta, **14**
Cha Cha Cha, **1**
Crescent City Cafe, **2**
Eliza's, **12**
Fillmore Grind, **4**

Hayes Street Grill, **16**
Horseshoe, **5**
It's Tops, **13**
Mad Magda's Russian Tea Room, **9**
Millenium, **21**

Miss Pearl's Jam House, **20**
Momi Toby's Revolution Cafe, **10**
Powell's Soul Food, **11**
Squat and Gobble Cafe, **6**
Stars, **19**

Suppenkuche, **8**
Tassajara Bread Bakery, **3**
Thep Phenom, **7**
Vicolo, **17**
Zuni Café, **18**

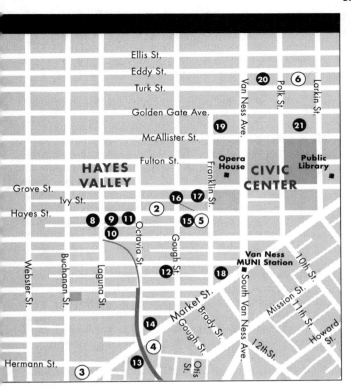

Scenes ○
Club
Confidential, **6**
Hayes and
Vine, **5**
Marlena's, **2**
Martuni's, **4**
Mint, **3**
Trax, **1**

$$-$$$ ✕ **Zuni Café.** Past its prime but still synonymous in San Francisco with upscale gay dining, Zuni gets its share of celebs and movie moguls—you still have to call ahead for a table. The rustic dining room is decorated as it though it were in the Wine Country. A perfect meal: Start with Caesar salad (best on the planet), then sample a dozen oysters (best selection in the city), before moving on to the roast chicken for two (best bargain of the entrées). A few complain that Zuni is too costly for what it serves. ⊠ *1658 Market St.,* ☎ *415/552–2522.*

$$ ✕ **Cafe Delle Stelle.** This Hayes Valley pasta house is one of the city's best for a filling, reasonably inexpensive meal (the long lines attest to its popularity). Although you could survive on the rich Tuscan bread that comes with your meal, you'll want to sample the delicious homemade pastas and traditional Italian fare, ranging from porcini gnocchi to veal scallopini with creamy Gorgonzola sauce. If you can't get a table here, check out Stelline, a half-block north on Gough Street, which is run by the same folks. ⊠ *395 Hayes St.,* ☎ *415/252–1110.*

$$ ✕ **Cha Cha Cha.** Hungry in the Haight? Check out this noisy, festive eatery. One of the many excellent Caribbean and Latin American restaurants around town, this one has a Southwest twist. The tapas include plantains with black beans and sour cream, and barbecued pork quesadilla. Brace yourself for the long lines. ⊠ *1801 Haight St.,* ☎ *415/386–5758. No credit cards.*

$$ ✕ **Eliza's.** Inventive Cal-styled Hunan and Mandarin Chinese food has made this intimate restaurant reason enough to wander into the up-and-coming Potrero Hill neighborhood, though many consider the Civic Center/Hayes Valley branch (on Oak) to be superior. ⊠ *205 Oak St.,* ☎ *415/621–4819; 1457 18th St.,* ☎ *415/648–9999.*

$$ ✕ **Millennium.** Set inside the unassuming Abigail Hotel is one of the city's most creative vegetarian restaurants. All the food is low-fat, organic, and dairy free—the grilled vegetables, polenta, and risotto dishes are terrific. You can sample meat substitutes, such as *seitan,* a shoe-leathery wad of whole wheat that's meant to resemble steak. The less-adventurous dishes are the safest. ⊠ *246 McAllister St.,* ☎ *415/487–9800.*

$$ ✕ **Miss Pearl's Jam House.** An adjunct to the funky Phoenix Hotel, Miss Pearl's gives diners in the culinarily challenged Tenderloin something to sink their teeth into. Jerk chicken and yam fries are competent interpretations of Caribbean food.

Lots of people come for the fruity cocktails, which are best sipped overlooking the Phoenix's memorable swimming pool. There's jammin' nightly in the adjacent bar. ⊠ *601 Eddy St.,* ☎ *415/775–5267.*

$$ ✕ **Suppenkuche.** If filling fare is your need, you won't be let down by the hearty sauerbraten, Wiener schnitzel, and smoked pork chops at this Old World wurst house with a huge selection of beers. ⊠ *601 Hayes St.,* ☎ *415/252–9289.*

$$ ✕ **Thep Phenom.** Off what unadventurous sorts call a dicey stretch of Lower Haight Street is one of the city's best Thai restaurants, with an elaborate menu, a lavish dining room filled with Thai art and antiques, and warm service. ⊠ *400 Waller St.,* ☎ *415/431–2526.*

$ ✕ **Crescent City Cafe.** Small and kinda greasy, this thread-bare spot serves outstanding Creole and Cajun fare, from oyster po'boys to andouille sausage hash. ⊠ *1418 Haight St.,* ☎ *415/863–1374.*

$ ✕ **It's Tops.** Though it bills itself as the original '50s diner, the look is more '70s—note the knotty-pine ceilings and walls, for instance. And how many '50s diners have espresso makers? There are, however, precious Seaburg Wall-O-Matic minijukes at every table. Typical diner food. ⊠ *1801 Market St.,* ☎ *415/431–6395. No credit cards.*

$ ✕ **Powell's Soul Food.** This place has been serving saucy ribs, smothered pork chops, and globs of mashed potatoes and collared greens for a couple of decades, long before the first yuppie moved into the Hayes Valley. Best R&B jukebox in town. ⊠ *511 Hayes St.,* ☎ *415/863–1404.*

$ ✕ **Squat and Gobble Café.** Okay, there's something vaguely unappetizing about the name of this funky breakfast and lunch hall just off lower Haight Street. But the crowd—a mix of shaggy-looking straights and queers—loves the hefty crepes and omelets. ⊠ *237 Fillmore St.,* ☎ *415/487–0551. No credit cards.*

$ ✕ **Vicolo.** This noisy pink-and-peach dining room churns out the most inventive pizza in town. The place may be guilty of overkill on the toppings—the "olive" pizza has mozzarella, fontina, red onion, green and calamata olives, Parmesan, garlic, and parsley—but everything tastes delicious. Slices are prepared and baked on the spot, so expect a 10-minute wait after placing your order. Plenty of beautiful people. ⊠ *201 Ivy St.,* ☎ *415/863–2382.*

Downtown and North Beach

$$$$ ✕ **Masa's.** Despite the constant praise this restaurant receives, the service remains refined and its ambience unstuffy. You can opt for the degustation menu or the menu du jour, which is slightly less costly. A sample degustation might include foie gras ravioli in a pheasant consommé with truffles, and a dessert of chocolate-pistachio terrine. ✉ *648 Bush St.,* ☎ *415/989–7154.*

$$$$ ✕ **Ritz-Carlton Dining Room.** This is a formal, elegant restaurant in a formal, elegant hotel. Gary Danko's exquisite cuisine—such as the quail salad with foie gras croutons and apricot-ginger chutney—suits the dapper setting perfectly; the service is positively doting. Danko is among the highest-profile gay chefs in the country. If last night's trick was a treat, consider bringing him or her to the ear-pleasing, eye-popping Sunday jazz brunch, where champagne, caviar, blintzes, and hazelnut tortes are culinary delights. ✉ *600 Stockton St.,* ☎ *415/296–7465.*

$$$$ ✕ **Tommy Toy's.** Taking a date to Tommy Toy's is like a really expensive gag gift. The French-influenced Chinese food is usually decent but overwrought to the point of being amusing (seafood bisque is served in an open coconut and topped with a puff pastry). The interior is like a scene from a Japanese mob film, with red carpets, tuxedo-clad waiters whisking about, no windows, and power deals going on all around you. One of those only-in-San Francisco (also one of those only-when-the-boss-is-paying) experiences. ✉ *655 Montgomery St.,* ☎ *415/397–4888.*

$$$– ✕ **Aqua.** Most Americans live a lifetime without sampling
$$$$ the caliber of seafood served amid explosively vibrant floral arrangements and elegant furnishings. Supremely fresh, its preparation is incredibly original, rooted in French and American traditions but always with an eye-opening twist: The rare *ahi* tuna comes with foie gras, and the delicious soufflées are made of mussels or lobster. ✉ *252 California St.,* ☎ *415/956–9662.*

$$$– ✕ **Cypress Club.** This off-the-wall supper club is known for
$$$$ its swank patrons, live jazz entertainment, and freewheeling New American cooking. The lobster soufflé is memorable. The Cypress Club is the brainchild of John Cunin, who opened 2223 in the Castro. ✉ *500 Jackson St.,* ☎ *415/296–8555.*

$$$–
$$$$ ✗ **One Market.** With nice views of San Francisco Bay and Justin Herman Plaza, this understated, formal, split-level dining room has banquette seating, views into the open kitchen, and piano entertainment most nights. The dishes on the eclectic menu have one common denominator: creativity. Consider the fried-onion salad with maple-smoked salmon and creamy chervil dressing, or the steamed Thai snapper with preserved lemon-ginger vinaigrette and vegetable couscous. ✉ *1 Market St.,* ☎ *415/777–5577.*

$$$ ✗ **Cafe Jacqueline.** What could be more romantic than sharing a rich soufflé with your lover in an intimate French bistro with high ceilings and crisp white linens. Chef Jacqueline is usually here, overseeing the considerably gay staff, who will explain this unusual dining concept: Soufflés for two are the only dishes available, either sweet (like white chocolate with fresh blueberries) or savory (like Gruyère, garlic, and prosciutto). In a hurry? This is not the place for you. ✉ *1454 Grant Ave.,* ☎ *415/981–5565.*

$$$ ✗ **Postrio.** Although it's a tad overrated, this creation and part-time home of celebrity-chef Wolfgang Puck still makes for a memorable dining experience. In the main dining room the crispy Chinese duck is a specialty. Consider saving a few bucks by eating in the bar; its menu shows off Puck's signature designer pizzas. Wherever you sit, prepare to watch a lot of moving and shaking. You'll have to call at least a week ahead for a table in the main room. ✉ *545 Post St.,* ☎ *415/776–7825.*

$$$ ✗ **Rubicon.** Backed by such investors as Robin Williams and Robert de Niro, lesbian and award-winning chef Traci des Jardins wows diners with her contemporary French fare. The setting is a stately stone building that dates from 1908. Fine regional wine list. ✉ *558 Sacramento St.,* ☎ *415/434–4100.*

$$$ ✗ **Splendido's.** Any of sunny Splendido's several rustic dining rooms provides the perfect place to enjoy a romantic dinner. The menu is largely southern French and northern Italian; try the chicken saltimbocca with wild rice, designer pizzas, warm goat cheese and ratatouille salad, or oak-roasted clams with smoked bacon. Great bay views. ✉ *Embarcadero 4,* ☎ *415/986–3222.*

$$–$$$ ✗ **Bix.** If you're not from a big city, you'll truly feel like you've arrived upon stepping into this Cotton Club–inspired supper club down an alley in the Financial District. The two-story open dining room makes for a magnificent setting in which to enjoy

42

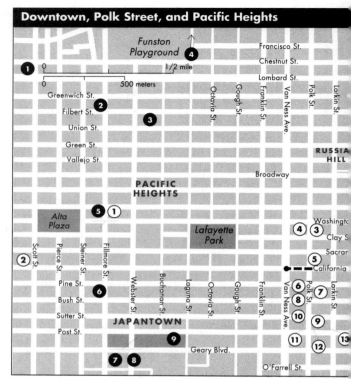

Downtown, Polk Street, and Pacific Heights

Funston Playground 4

Francisco St.
Chestnut St.
Lombard St.
Greenwich St. 2
Filbert St. 3
Union St.
Green St.
Vallejo St.

Octavia St.
Gough St.
Franklin St.
Van Ness Ave.
Polk St.
Larkin St.

RUSSIAN HILL

Broadway

PACIFIC HEIGHTS

Alta Plaza 5 1

Lafayette Park

Washington
4 3 Clay St.
5 Sacramento
California

Scott St.
Pierce St.
Steiner St.
Fillmore St.

Pine St. 6
Bush St.
Sutter St.
Post St.

Webster St.
Buchanan St.
Laguna St.
Octavia St.
Gough St.
Franklin St.
Van Ness Ave.
Polk St.
Larkin St.

6 7
8
10 9
11 12 13

JAPANTOWN

9

Geary Blvd.

O'Farrell St.

1/2 mile
500 meters

Eats ●
Alta Plaza, **5**
Aqua, **30**
Betelnut, **3**
Bix, **19**
Café Akimbo, **26**
Cafe Jacqueline, **14**
Cafe Marimba, **1**

Cafe Tiramisu, **28**
Caffe Trieste, **16**
Cypress Club, **18**
Dottie's True Blue Cafe, **11**
Emporio Armani Express Café, **27**
Greens, **4**

House of Nanking, **17**
Isobune, **7**
Lori's, **25**
Mario's Bohemian Cigar Store, **12**
Masa's, **22**
Mifune, **8**

North Beach Pizza, **13**
One Market, **32**
Oritalia, **6**
Plump Jack Café, **2**
Postrio, **24**
Ritz-Carlton Dining Room, **21**

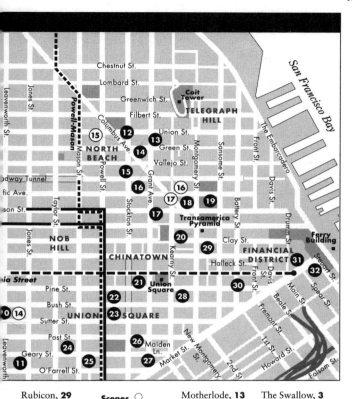

Rubicon, **29**
Scala's, **23**
Splendido's, **31**
Titanic Cafe, **10**
Tommy Toy's, **20**
U.S. Restaurant, **15**
Yoyo, **9**

Scenes ○
Alta Plaza, **1**
Beach Blanket Babylon, **15**
Cinch Saloon, **4**
Finocchio's, **16**
The Giraffe, **10**
Kimo's, **6**
Lion Pub, **2**

Motherlode, **13**
N'Touch, **5**
Polk Gulch, **12**
Polk Rendezvous, **8**
P.S. Bar, **11**
QT, **7**
Red Room, **14**
Reflections, **9**

The Swallow, **3**
Tosca, **17**

the likes of lobster ravioli and other Continental and New American favorites. At the very least drop in for one of the trademark martinis. ⊠ *56 Gold St.,* ☎ *415/433–6300.*

$$ ✕ **Café Akimbo.** A certain well-respected dining guidebook describes Café Akimbo as being "popular with ladies who shop." This could not be more true––the place is absolutely crawling with designer fags. Mondrianesque walls colored with muted jewel tones create a stylish dining room known for such creative seafood fare as spring rolls filled with enoki and shiitake mushrooms in a tangy mango sauce. With many dishes around $10, it's a steal. Bring along your compass; it's tricky to find. ⊠ *116 Maiden La.,* ☎ *415/433–2288.*

$$ ✕ **Cafe Tiramisu.** This charming sidewalk café takes the corporate edge off of all those Financial District stockbrokers— still, you'll witness a lot of intense power-lunch dates here. You can't go wrong with any of the salads. Save room for the splendid tiramisu. ⊠ *28 Belden St.,* ☎ *415/421–7044.*

$$ ✕ **Emporio Armani Express Café.** A good spot for celeb spotting, preening and posing, and browsing for fashionable duds, Armani's café floats on a mezzanine in the center of a huge retail space. You sit at the bar within an arm's reach of the clothing. Whereas Armani threads sometimes prosper on reputation alone, this food is genuinely tasty, from light pizzas with creative toppings to heavenly sandwiches, pastas, and salads. ⊠ *1 Grant Ave.,* ☎ *415/677–9010.*

$$ ✕ **Scala's.** One of those handsome old-fashioned restaurants that seems to have inspired the phrase "let's do lunch," Scala's draws a relatively high number of gays, at least compared with other Union Square–area establishments. The northern Italian and southern French food is consistently good, including braised lamb shank and rotisserie chicken. ⊠ *432 Powell St.,* ☎ *415/395–8555.*

$–$$ ✕ **North Beach Pizza.** Not only touristy, this place is often populated by slightly horrifying mobs of straight kids from the suburbs. Still, the maroon vinyl booths and green Formica tables are refreshingly ungentrified, and the pizza is otherworldly. The pies are huge—two slices is plenty for most people. ⊠ *1499 Grant Ave.,* ☎ *415/433–2444.*

$–$$ ✕ **U.S. Restaurant.** This is an authentic short-order North Beach diner where ancient waitresses and Italian-speaking cooks yuk it up with their customers, who include cops, old-time locals, yuppies, and a smattering of tourists. Every night has a featured special; two of the best are Tuesday's lasagna

and Friday's fried calamari. The portions are truly family size.
⊠ *431 Columbus Ave.,* ☎ *415/362–6251.*

$ ✗ **Dottie's True Blue Cafe.** It's just off Union Square, seats perhaps two-dozen people, and may not look like much, but Dottie's is a San Francisco fixture when it comes to filling breakfast fare and homestyle lunches. Pretty gay by Union Square standards. ⊠ *522 Jones St.,* ☎ *415/885–2767.*

$ ✗ **House of Nanking.** This no-frills restaurant has perfunctory service and suffers from long lines, but it's still one of the better places to eat in Chinatown. A plate of heavenly shrimp cakes in peanut sauce or light vegetable dumplings will make you glad you came. ⊠ *919 Kearny St.,* ☎ *415/421–1429. No credit cards.*

$ ✗ **Lori's.** You'll be thankful for this 24-hour diner near Union Square if you're clubbed-out, on your way back to your hotel, and still hungry. Decorated with '50s memorabilia, Marilyn Monroe photos, red-glitter vinyl seats, and art deco sconces, the setting will wake you up fast. Enjoy great burgers, vanilla malts, and unusually ungreasy fries. ⊠ *336 Mason St.,* ☎ *415/392–8646.*

$ ✗ **Mario's Bohemian Cigar Store.** Just off Washington Park is one of the few eateries in North Beach where a couple of same-sexers can comfortably hold hands on a date. Nobody here will care, as gawking tourists (most of whom can't figure out this quirky, misnamed café—they don't sell cigars) are few and far between. Come for pure Italian food, like roasted eggplant or meatball sandwiches. Bring an extra belt to rein yourself in after a bite of ricotta cheesecake. ⊠ *566 Columbus Ave.,* ☎ *415/362–0536. No credit cards.*

$ ✗ **Titanic Cafe.** With an oceanic color scheme and fish tanks and bowls arranged strategically throughout, this tiny coffee shop in the ultracool Commodore hotel will leave you with a renewed appreciation for cruise-ship kitsch. Lunch and breakfast are the only meals concocted in the Titanic's galley, but the fare is like none you'll find on most ships, or in most hotel coffee shops, for that matter: buckwheat griddlecakes, Vietnamese tofu sandwiches, and other healthful, inventive plates. ⊠ *817 Sutter St.,* ☎ *415/928–8870. No credit cards.*

West of Van Ness

$$$ ✗ **Yoyo.** A princess of San Francisco's lesbian culinary elite, Elka Gilmore, oversees this chic Pan-Asian seafood restaurant at the Miyako Hotel. The dining room's colorful murals provide an appropriate backdrop for such fare as the salmon with soba noodles, bonita flakes, and shiitake consommé, and the squab with balsamic figs and port sauce. Japanese-style smaller plates are also featured; they're great for nibbling. ✉ *1625 Post St.,* ☎ *415/922–7788.*

$$–$$$ ✕ **Alta Plaza.** If you've always thought of the Alta Plaza first as a guppity gay bar and then as a mediocre New American restaurant, think again. Chef Amey Shaw has attracted a new following by cooking up a global storm of tasty cuisine. Favorites include marinated teriyaki-roasted lamb riblets with a spicy mustard sauce and a risotto with golden chanterelle, shiitake, and lobster mushrooms, drizzled with white truffle oil. ✉ *2301 Fillmore St.,* ☎ *415/922–1444.*

$$–$$$ ✕ **Cafe Marimba.** Come here for the city's most authentic Oaxacan and Zihuatenejan cooking; it's a pleasant contrast to heavier Sonoran Mexican food. Everything is prepared as it is in Mexico (note the dry-roasted tomatoes and peppers). Tamales with a mole negro sauce are a specialty of the house. With 26 brands of tequila, you can expect mouthwatering margaritas. ✉ *2317 Chestnut St.,* ☎ *415/776–1506.*

$$–$$$ ✕ **Greens.** It's a haul from any of the more interesting neighborhoods, but this innovative vegetarian restaurant has been turning heads for years. On weekends you can only order the five-course prix-fixe dinner; it's famous among food lovers nationwide and is a bargain when you consider the caliber of cooking. Be sure to sample the bakery's fresh bread and pastries. ✉ *Bldg. A, Fort Mason,* ☎ *415/771–6222.*

$$–$$$ ✕ **Oritalia.** Marble floors, black-and-gold pillars, wood paneling, and generous use of mirrors give this Pacific Heights dining room the look of a chic trattoria. But as its name hints, Oritalia combines Italian and exotic Asian influences. Half the fun is witnessing the artful presentation; the rest is devouring it. Consider rock shrimp, cilantro, ginger, cream, and tobiko, or the grilled portobello mushrooms with plum wine jus. ✉ *1915 Fillmore St.,* ☎ *415/346–1333.*

$$–$$$ ✕ **PlumpJack Café.** One of the best of Cow Hollow's several slick bistros serves fine California cuisine, with an emphasis on fresh seafood and meat grills. It's affiliated with the nearby wine shop of the same name, which accounts for the more than 30 vintages of wine by the glass. ✉ *3127 Fillmore St.,* ☎ *415/563–4755.*

$–$$ ✕ **Betelnut.** Varied and surprising marriages of cuisine span-
ning the Orient have made this relatively young study in bam-
boo and lacquered walls worth a trip to Cow Hollow. Some
of the unusual food, which emphasizes small plates, includes
stir-fried anchovies, chilies, peanuts, garlic, and scallions, and
a light papaya salad. ✉ *2026 Union St.,* ☎ *415/929–8855.*

$–$$ ✕ **Isobune.** Stop in here for inexpensive sushi. Favorites
such as octopus and salmon roe are unbelievably fresh; the
food floats by you on little wooden boats along a counter-
top moat—you pluck whatever interests you. ✉ *1737 Post
St.,* ☎ *415/563–1030.*

$–$$ ✕ **Mifune.** For fresh, authentic soba and udon noodles head
to this Japan Center restaurant where a full dinner typically
weighs in at under $6. ✉ *Kintetsu Bldg., 1737 Post St.,* ☎
415/922–0337.

Richmond and Sunset Districts

$$$ ✕ **Alain Rondelli.** One of S.F.'s culinary stars folds Asian and
Latin American touches into contemporary French dishes.
The atmosphere is quiet and romantic. Desserts are exquisite,
and the wine list has been shrewdly chosen. ✉ *126 Clement
St.,* ☎ *415/387–0408.*

$$ ✕ **Casa Aguila.** You'll have to head way over to Sunset for
the city's most amazing burritos, rich chicken mole, and
spicy salsa. This little neighborhood joint has developed a
big following, so you can expect long lines on weekend afternoons. You may want to finish your spicy meal with a dish
of tropical ice cream. ✉ *1240 Noriega St.,* ☎ *415/661–5593.*

$–$$ ✕ **Le Soleil.** Author Amy Tan is among those who have dined
at this stylish Vietnamese restaurant. Try the rice-flour crepe
with bean sprouts, chicken, and shrimp for an appetizer.
Mint leaves add zest to several salads. Several clay pot dishes
are inventively prepared. Service can be slow, so don't come
here if you're in a hurry. ✉ *133 Clement St.,* ☎ *415/668–
4848.*

$–$$ ✕ **Ton Kiang.** A great choice for Hakka cuisine (from south-
ern China) is also one of San Francisco's best dim-sum
palaces. The kitchen turns out great variations on traditional
dim sum, many of them employing seafood. If you've a yen
for the old standbys—chicken feet, duck tongue, and the like—
you'll find them, too. A sister restaurant at 3148 Geary is

closer to downtown, but the quality here is a notch higher. ⊠ *5821 Geary Blvd.,* ☎ *415/387–8273.*

Coffeehouse Culture

The Castro

Cafe Flore. Heading into its third decade of caffeinating the Castro's queers, Café Hairdo (as it's often teased) is San Francisco's gay ground zero. You can come for breakfast, stay through lunch, stick around for afternoon coffee, grab a beer before dinner, eat dinner, and finish things off with cordials and dessert. It's true, you never have to leave—some never do. ⊠ *2298 Market St.,* ☎ *415/621–8579.*

Castro Country Club. This casual spot originated in 1983 as a nonalcoholic alternative to the area's many bars. It remains a pressure-free place for clean-and-sober rendezvous. ⊠ *4058 18th St.,* ☎ *415/552–6102.*

Jumpin' Java. This laid-back dykey coffeehouse is right in the heart of the Market Street action and serves decent salads and light fare. A good spot to arrange to meet friends, it's not as much of a scene as Cafe Flore. ⊠ *139 Noe St.,* ☎ *415/431–5282.*

Just Desserts. Chomp on pies, pastries, and heavenly cheesecake at this purveyor of things fattening and delicious. ⊠ *248 Church St.,* ☎ *415/626–5774.*

Pasqua. Though part of the chain, this Pasqua is highly queer—in a bronzed-and-buffed sort of way. ⊠ *Castro and 18th Sts.,* ☎ *415/626–6263.*

Mission District

Cafe Commons. The space on the ground-floor of this attractive, three-story, teal-painted building draws a retro thrift-shop crowd. It has a patio, an espresso bar, and a typical soup, quiche, and sandwich menu. ⊠ *3161 Mission St.,* ☎ *415/282–2928.*

Muddy's Coffee House. These lesbian-favored beaneries have a couple of outdoor tables and get a good mix of locals, artists, and queers. Both establishments have bright, airy main rooms with good people-watching vistas. ⊠ *510 Valenica St.,* ☎ *415/863–8006; 1304 Valencia St.,* ☎ *415/647–7994.*

Red Dora's Bearded Lady Café. You can get great bagels, veggie burritos, and other meatless fare at this divinely dykey, hip, smoke-free, PC lesbian performance space. The votive candles are a nice touch. ⊠ *485 14th St.,* ☎ *415/626–2805.*

Civic Center, Hayes Valley, and the Haight

Fillmore Grind. This cheerful coffeehouse in an up-and-coming area between Alamo Square and Hayes Valley always draws a diverse crowd. Not a scene like many of its Castro counterparts, the Grind is a good place to meet with a friend for a quiet cup of java. ⊠ *711 Fillmore St.,* ☎ *415/775–5680.*

Horseshoe. If you're toddling around the Lower Haight, you may want to pop your head inside the Horseshoe. Unless your head has been shaved, tattooed, pierced, or dyed an electric color, you may feel completely out of place—but that's part of the fun. ⊠ *566 Haight St.,* ☎ *415/626–8852.*

Mad Magda's Russian Tea Room. One of the more eccentric hangouts in Hayes Valley has an unaffected bohemian feel. You can have a tarot card reading while enjoying some of the best sandwiches (like the Fabergé eggplant with mozzarella and basil) in town. Live music many nights. ⊠ *579 Hayes St.,* ☎ *415/864–7654.*

Momi Toby's Revolution Cafe. This is the place to bring your dog (or chat with some cutie who's brought one along) on weekend mornings and afternoons. It's so cozy it almost feels like somebody's house. Sketchbooks, markers, and crayons are provided to keep you busy. Comfort food is served all day long. ⊠ *528 Laguna St.,* ☎ *415/626–1508.*

Tassajara Bread Bakery. Before the exemplary local chain of sweets shops, Just Desserts, purchased it a few years back, this Cole Valley (near Upper Haight) institution was run by Zen monks. Many locals claim they can still channel the monks' energy when biting into the bakery's stellar muffins, croissants, and scones. The atmosphere is warm and neighborly, especially on weekend mornings, when regulars sip coffee or organic tea while reading the paper. ⊠ *1000 Cole St.,* ☎ *415/664–8947.*

North Beach

Caffe Trieste. Beat poet Allen Ginsberg and his pack regularly graced the tables of this North Beach institution. The Giotta family has run the place since it opened in 1956, cultivating a warm but definitely not fancy atmosphere in which to sip a cappuccino. ⊠ *601 Vallejo St.,* ☎ *415/392–6739.*

SoMa

Caffé Centro. This spring-day-in-Paris-looking coffeehouse, set in a yellow-and-lime clapboard house overlooking shady South Park, is not to be missed. Not only is the ambience a

form of sustenance, but the fresh salads, sandwiches, and pastries will warm your soul and fill your stomach. An added bonus is the promise of meeting some cute Web-page creator taking a break from one of this neighborhood's many computer-design firms. ✉ *102 South Park Ave.,* ☎ *415/882–1500.*
Palette Cafe. Just steps from Rough Trade records, this postmodern art gallery, café, and beanery near China Basin serves baked goods, vegetarian sandwiches, and salads. ✉ *699 3rd St.,* ☎ *415/896–0844.*

SCENES

The quality of San Francisco's nightlife is a touchy subject. On the one hand, you'll hear people describing it as an older and fairly tired scene. On the other, you'll be reminded that the city may have more gay bars per capita than any other place in the world. Of course, if you think about it, these two views are not mutually exclusive. San Francisco does in fact have about 80 gay bars and only about 750,000 residents. New York City has fewer gay bars and about 10 times the population. However, be forewarned that quantity does not guarantee variety.

About 50 of the city's gay bars are small and sleepy, catering mostly to old drunks. This doesn't mean that these places aren't fun, or that you can't meet people in them. It's just that . . . well, there are times when you could swear that the guy across the room is staring at you because he has the hots for you. So maybe you smile back at him—you know, with one eyebrow arched. And he keeps staring. So you're feeling a little bold tonight; you walk over to him and introduce yourself. And, still, he just keeps staring. So, finally, you give him a quick tap on the shoulder, just to see if anybody is in there. And crash! He falls off his bar stool.

San Francisco had a wild and crazy '70s, and a rough '80s. If you check out the bars along lower Polk Street and in the Tenderloin, you're going to see a lot of the walking wounded. By the early '90s the time-honored S.F. fag-bar traditions of lust and licentiousness had lost their vigor. It seemed sometimes as though younger queers, especially male ones, were no longer settling here in great numbers. Recent years have seen more age diversity, and several largely straight clubs and smaller bars have developed mixed followings, with music, fashion, and mood being more the uniting social forces than sexual orientation. That's not to say you can't get laid at these places, only that cruising—the sole priority at many Castro bars—sometimes takes a back seat to mingling.

The city's most interesting (or at least characterful) spots are described in detail below. Within this grouping you'll find just about every type of watering hole known to humanity: leather, guppie, piano, sports, Latino, Asian, African-American, warehouse disco, drag, strip club—you name it.

The narrator of the late-1960s mock documentary *Gay San Francisco*, sounding something like an anthropologist in the wilds of Borneo, had this loopy assessment of the after-dark predilections of S.F.'s gay women: "Lesbians don't hit the bars . . . they tend to gather in tight-knit social groups." Whatever the truth was 30 years ago, one might have supposed that the scene would have picked up, but even today only one full-time lesbian bar exists—which does seem strange for such a dykey city. Making up for their absence, however, are cafés, weekly roving girl parties, and women's performance spaces—a visiting lesbian can definitely have a good time here.

All in all San Francisco does have a lively nightlife. You may have to forage to find your ideal crowd, but somewhere there's a bar stool or party chair with your name on it. All you have to do is try not to fall off it.

The Castro and the Mission

PRIME SUSPECTS

Badlands. This is a terrific place for both its eclectic selection of tunes, from oldies to rock to disco, and for its collection of oddly monogrammed license plates. A little larger than its neighbors, the Badlands fills up quickly, especially on Sundays. The decorating scheme is vaguely Southwest—chaps and cattle skulls—and there are pool tables and many pinball machines. Chatty, handsome bartenders. ⊠ *4121 18th St.,* ☎ *415/626–9320. Crowd: mostly male, 20s and 30s, lots of flannel and denim, cruisy, cute but unpretentious.*
The Cafe. The Castro's most—some would say only—happening dance club just gets more and more popular with each passing year. The Cafe opened as a lesbian bar, but pretty soon the boys realized that it's a much nicer space than most

of their clubs, so now it's pretty mixed. You enter up a flight of stairs to festive bars, one on your right and another up more stairs to your left. At two always-in-use pool tables, the women generally prove that The Cafe is, in fact, their turf. A tiny dance floor manages to accommodate several dozen hip-shakers. The walls are lined with big windows, and on one side a great little balcony overlooks Market, Castro, and 17th streets. The best mingling space is a wooden deck that's also a good spot to cool off or stargaze with a new friend. ⊠ *2367 Market St.,* ☎ *415/861–3846. Crowd: mixed m/f, baby dykes, club kids, college students, guppies, fashion plates, sometimes a bit too cliquey.*

Castro Station. In addition to many Tom of Finland-type works on the walls here, several odd objets d'art pay homage to the bar's train-station theme. These items include an ersatz stained-glass locomotive and a neon speeding diesel engine. Neat. ⊠ *456 Castro St.,* ☎ *415/626–7220. Crowd: mostly male, all ages, all races, zero attitude, cruisy but mellow.*

Daddy's. If you're lucky, you'll catch this place on a night when they're screening *Planet of the Apes* reruns. Other times they show campy old films or sporting events. The crowd is on the bearish side, but in a warm, fuzzy, intoxicated sort of way. There's a deck off the back of a narrow front room with a bar, a pool table, and pinball machines. ⊠ *440 Castro St.,* ☎ *415/621–8732. Crowd: 75/25 m/f; mostly fortysomething; lots of facial hair, chest hair, back hair; fairly butch but down-to-earth.*

Detour. Little about the Castro's tried-and-true pickup bar has changed over the years, except that the extensive chain-link fencing may be getting a little rusty (along with a few of the guys). The Detour has precious little open space, which forces guys to brush up against one another. The pool table up front is constantly in use, apparently even when the bar is closed— a couple of years ago Falcon Studios filmed a porn flick on top of it. ⊠ *2348 Market St.,* ☎ *415/861–6053. Crowd: male, mostly under 35, a sea of denim and white T-shirts.*

The Edge. This casual bar has an "edge of the universe" motif, with a glow-in-the-dark model of our solar system laid out against the ceiling—much like your bedroom might have looked when you were a child. This and the free peanuts are the bar's only distinguishing features. Nevertheless, there's always a substantial crowd. ⊠ *4149 18th St.,* ☎ *415/863–*

4027. *Crowd: mostly male, thirtysomething, on their way to or from other Castro bars.*

El Rio. On Sunday afternoons this Mission dive dishes up live salsa music and great food—it's one of the liveliest parties in the city. The rest of the time El Rio combines the best attributes of a disco, a pool hall, and a restaurant. The back patio is a great space on warm days. Queer women of color flock to the Saturday-night Red party. ☒ *3158 Mission St.,* ☎ *415/282–3325. Crowd: totally mixed gay/straight, male/female; Latino, African-American, white; old, young.*

Esta Noche. A fixture since the '70s, the city's main queer Latin disco still rages. It's a great place to dance, watch the campy drag shows on Wednesday nights, and make a lot of noise. The crowd is young and insular, so don't be shy. ☒ *3079 16th St.,* ☎ *415/861–5757. Crowd: mostly male, mostly Latino, young, loud, raucous.*

Harvey's. The former Elephant Walk is now named for the late activist Harvey Milk. Appropriately, the walls are covered with memorabilia tracing Milk's life and the history of San Francisco's gay community. Plate-glass windows overlook the cruisy intersection of Castro and 18th. The space has been refurbished with a spiffy contemporary look. In addition to the usual brews, you can test out hard-to-find wines, vodkas, tequilas, cognacs, single-malt Scotches, and liqueurs. ☒ *500 Castro St.,* ☎ *415/431–4278. Crowd: mixed gay/lesbian, all ages, friendly, low-key, not at all cruisy.*

The Lexington Club. A very cool dyke bar opened in the Mission District in early 1997. A hip grrrl crowd packs the cozy space to hear Joan Jett and Courtney Love tunes on the fierce jukebox. This site has been home to several non-lesbian bars over the years, so it's not uncommon to see a few older Latin men bending an elbow among the crowd of skater girls, hipsters, and Doc Marten devotees. ☒ *3464 19th St.,* ☎ *415/863–2052. Crowd: 80/20 f/m, young, stylish, sexy, unpretentious, loud.*

Metro. It's hard to know what to make of this neon-infused and dated-looking bar. Were it not for its mysteriously mobbed Tuesday karaoke nights and its balcony overlooking Noe, Market, and 16th streets, nobody might venture in here. The weeknight early-evening happy hours and weekend afternoons are also well attended. ☒ *3600 16th St,,* ☎ *415/703–9750. Crowd: 65/35 m/f, diverse in every other way.*

Midnight Sun. This cruisy midsize video bar is probably the safest bet for tourists hoping to find boys just like the ones back home. Music videos, campy movie clips, and fag favorites such as *Ab Fab* flicker on several TV screens as dance music blares overhead. Has declined slightly in popularity. ⊠ *4067 18th St.,* ☎ *415/861–4186. Crowd: mostly male; young, clean-shaven; professional, like the boys at Alta Plaza but without high-paying jobs.*

Moby Dick. The claims to fame here are a huge tropical-fish tank and the literary moniker, which almost begs you to go up to the first cute guy you see, tell him your name, smile, and declare: ". . . but you, my friend, may call me Ishmael." Basically, Moby Dick is a video bar with a pool table, pinball, and all the usual diversions. Sometimes people refer to it unkindly by exchanging the word "Moby" with "Moldy." ⊠ *4049 18th St., no phone. Crowd: mostly male, thirtysomething, a bit sleazier but otherwise similar to the guys at the Midnight Sun.*

Pendulum. This is San Francisco's only African-American bar, though men of color patronize many other spots. Inside, the bar looks like a party room in a frat house, packed with a rowdy, outgoing bunch. Cruisy bathroom. The Pendulum been around for more than 25 years. ⊠ *4146 18th St.,* ☎ *415/863– 4441. Crowd: mostly male, mostly African-American, all ages, all types, very friendly.*

Phoenix. The Castro's oldest dance hall has a bar in front and a tiny dance floor in back. You'll get dizzy with the abundance of disco balls, strobe lights, and I-beams—the accompanying music and videos are fun, if a little dated. Gets a very young crowd, so young that the Phoenix has become about the only club in the Castro to card everybody. ⊠ *482 Castro St.,* ☎ *415/552–6827. Crowd: 85/15 m/f, either very young men of color or older men of no color.*

Twin Peaks. This was the first bar in the nation to have clear street-level windows, thereby allowing curious straight people to observe us up close, in our native environment. It opened in 1972, and because it attracts many of the Castro's old-timers, bitchy young people often call it a "wrinkle bar." It's also called a "fern bar," although there are no ferns. In any case it's a cheerful haunt with Tiffany-style lamps and a crowd that seems to know one another on a first-name basis. Its best attribute is the intimate interior balcony, where lovers

who are coping (fighting) often go to process (break up). ⌧
401 Castro St., ☎ *415/864–9470. Crowd: mostly male, 35
to 75, cordial, white-collar, a bit cliquey.*

It seems almost unkind for gays to overwhelm the one predominantly straight club in (actually on the fringe of) the
Castro, but **Cafe du Nord** (⌧ 2170 Market St., ☎ 415/861–
5016) is too much fun to miss. A moody basement of red
carpets and dark-wood tables and chairs, du Nord books a
lineup of polished jazz musicians and has great cabaret
shows. It's not really fair to call this a straight or gay bar,
anyway. All types hang here; a modicum of sophistication
is the only prerequisite.

Along the same lines, in SoMa (*see below*) the larger clubs
go back and forth, gay then straight, and so on. It's a pain
keeping up with it all, and these days you can't tell a genXer's
inclinations from his or her nail polish anyhow. So why try?
You may as well tread over to the Mission District, where
slinky noir **Dalva** (⌧ 3121 16th St., ☎ 415/252–7740)
draws a skulking potpourri of genderbenders and pansexu-
als. The atmosphere is very *not there,* meaning bare cement
floors and lighting that paints everybody in a German Expressionist glow. Bring your European cigarettes (Canadian
will do in a pinch) and prepare to mix and match. It can get
cliquey in here, not to the point that loners feel out of place,
only that they're likely to remain loners as the night dwin-
dles to a murmur.

Things don't get much sleepier than they do at the **Men's Room**
(⌧ 3988 18th St., ☎ 415/861–1310), which behind its
cedar-shake exterior has a long bar that's short on customers.
Ditto for chummy, slightly more crowded **Uncle Bert's** (⌧
4086 18th St., ☎ 415/431–8616), where they've been known
to show televised golf on Saturday nights.

Cute and stylish genXers and nostalgic thirtysomethings sat-
isfy their retro music needs Wednesday nights at **Baby Judy's**
(⌧ Casanova, 527 Valencia St., ☎ 415/863–9328), a Mission District party whose mission is to see that everyone learns
how to "walk liiiike . . . an eeh gyp shun," among other
underappreciated party skills. Wholesome fun for everyone.

Tuesdays at Casanova are also quite a romp, when **Starfucker** shifts into high gear with camp film classics and a salon-meets-club-kid scene.

SoMa

PRIME SUSPECTS

Hole in the Wall Saloon. The self-proclaimed "Nasty Little Biker Bar" is aptly named—it's a hellish sliver of a place where they play hard-rock music and the guys throw each other deadly looks. If you're lucky, a fight will break out during your visit. If you want to increase the odds of this happening, wear a polo shirt and plenty of cologne. The doors open at 6 AM—gentlemen, start your engines. The bathroom has a narrow trough urinal with mirrors, which encourages sharing. One of the more artful touches is a mysterious towering blob of wax that's been growing above the bar counter since about 1977. Some of this place's edge has been lost as curiosity seekers have begun discovering its many charms, but it's still a whole lotta fun. ⊠ *289 8th St., ☎ 415/431–4695. Crowd: mostly male, often drunk by noon, lots of leather, piercings aplenty, a smattering of guppies.*

Rawhide II. Queer radicals with good memories won't set foot in this country-western bar whose owner once published a perhaps-too-conservative gay rag and, worse yet, rented the Rawhide out to the producers of the psycho-lesbo flick *Basic Instinct*. Still, it's the premier gay C&W joint in town, with a lodgelike decor—deer heads, cowboy memorabilia—and Nashville sounds. Every weeknight you can drop in for free dance lessons from 7:30 to 9:30; this is an easy way to meet people. ⊠ *280 7th St., ☎ 415/621–1197. Crowd: mixed m/f, serious western gear, great dancers, loud and outgoing.*

S.F. Eagle. The Sunday beer blast here is phenomenally popular. At other times this is one of the city's best leather bars—the guys here take the theme very seriously. There's even a great leather shop on the premises, one of the finest you'll find anywhere. Sometimes the place gets dark and cramped, but you can amble out onto the heated outdoor patio. Hmmm. These guys may not be so tough after all. ⊠ *398 12th St., ☎ 415/626–0880. Crowd: male, leather, brawny, butch; big, rough, he-man central.*

Stud. Yet another of the roving-party venues in SoMa is a tight and compact place with a narrow, crowded dance floor and several areas for mingling. The Stud has been hot for many years. The crowd, ambience, and musical flavor change according to the night. Mondays are funk; Tuesdays bring the tongue-in-cheek Trannyshack; Wednesdays, mostly male and on the young side, feature old disco favorites; and Thursdays are a tribute to white trash. At Low Rider on the first and third Saturday of the month, mostly boys dance to trip-hop and old school. Sunday's retro and new wave party is a load of fun. ✉ *399 9th St.,* ☎ *415/863–6623. Crowd: depends on the theme but tends to be young, low attitude, mixed genders, multiracial.*

V/SF. This multilevel club opened in 1996 to tremendous crowds. V/SF is *très* Eurodisco—very industrial, almost like a movie set, with a large dance space and more of those comfy leather booths on either side, plus a small pool room. The Eurotrash fantasy is ruined only by the realization that nobody is smoking; the dance floor is smoke-free (you are in San Francisco—you will lead a healthy life, damn it!). In the back of the club are two routes to a rooftop patio with outdoor furniture and potted greenery and ferns. Note: At press time (early 1997), V/SF was only open weekends (with fewer gay-themed nights), and an ominous "For Sale" sign had been slapped on the building. Check the gay rags before heading down. ✉ *278 11th St.,* ☎ *415/621–1530. Crowd: Varies from night to night, but youngish; fairly good racial mix.*

NEIGHBORHOOD HAUNTS

Although it's not a gay place per se, **Julie's Supper Club** (✉ 1123 Folsom St., ☎ 415/861–0707) has a reasonably queer following. It serves good food with a '50s take on futuristic decorating. You'll find lots of pre-clubbers sipping cocktails—the martinis have attained cult status.

The seedy **Lonestar** (✉ 1354 Harrison St., ☎ 415/863–9999) is called an "ego bar" by some, and that's not because everybody here has a big ego. **My Place** (✉ 1225 Folsom St., ☎ 415/863–2329) is one of the few leather bars in SoMa that still has back-room activity. **Powerhouse** (✉ 1347 Folsom St., ☎ 415/552–8689), once synonymous with hard-core leather, is becoming a hit with the pierced grunge set, especially for its Thursday night **Sissybar** parties.

ONE-NIGHTERS, MOVEABLE FETES

The Box. This Thursday-night funk-and-house dance party has been bringin' 'em in for nearly a decade. A room in the front has a balcony with lounge chairs and a small dance floor with great music. The larger dance hall has catwalks, a stage, and that ubiquitous postindustrial black-box-theater look. Above the main dance floor is a small bar, and off that a cozy space with two pool tables. DJ Page Hodel is a local legend; The Box has always lured a sizeable contingent of lesbians. ⊠ *715 Harrison St.,* ☎ *415/647–8258. Crowd: 75/25 m/f, straight-friendly, mostly mid-20s to mid-30s, from hard-core club goers to nostalgia-seeking couples reliving their younger years.*

After the Box, many of the diehards continue dancing until 6 AM the next morning at **Lift,** which is held at **Club DV8** (⊠ 55 Natoma St., ☎ 415/267–5984).

On Saturday nights the city's wildest, must-do parties are held at **Club Townsend** (⊠ 177 Townsend St., no phone). Most recently the party has been called **Club Universe** (☎ 415/985–5241), but should the name change you'll still be able to count on huge crowds that are young and wired—mostly male but some lesbians and straights. An enormous old warehouse, 177 Townsend has a large dance space and pulsates until 7 AM. Sunday nights, a long-running and largely male tea dance, **Pleasuredome** (☎ 415/985–5256), gets rolling around 10 PM. A women's party, **Club Q** (*see* Women's Bars and Hangouts, *below*), is held here the first Friday of every month.

On Fridays, dykes and gay men descend upon **Litter Box** (⊠ Cat's Grill and Alley Club, rear entrance, 683 Clementina St., ☎ 415/431–3332), a festive party of retro cuts and dance classics.

Featured prominently in *Tales of the City,* and constantly a source of gossip and speculation (Didn't it close? Is it about to close? Have new owners taken over?), the **End Up** (⊠ 401 Harrison St., ☎ 415/487–6277) has been a San Francisco treat since the early '70s. A throbbing tea dance revs its engine at 6 AM Sunday morning and rolls along until 6 in the evening—in good weather most people cut loose on the patio. The End Up also began throwing the mostly male Fag

Friday parties in 1996. The festivities begin with a beer bust at 10 PM and continue with go-go boys, dancing, and dishing well into the morning.

Although the N' Touch (*see below*) continues to be the city's only full-time gaysian club, **Asia** (✉ 174 King St., ☎ 415/974–6020), held in SoMa the second and fourth Fridays of every month, has fast become one of S.F.'s hottest queer events. The place fills up with a diverse bunch of men, usually at least half of Asian descent. Both the music and lighting are stellar.

Joining the current statewide trend of youth-oriented queer nightspots, **Special K** (✉ 800 Stevenson St., ☎ 415/436–0409) began its 18-and-over mostly gay-male dance parties in 1996. Every Saturday night this SoMa disco fills up with peach-fuzzy queerteens and older hawks looking to cash in on the club's decidedly sexy and youthful personality. It gets a little cliquey and attitudy in here, but the energy is high and the crowd pretty.

Polk Street

PRIME SUSPECTS

Cinch Saloon. Except for the music, which is culled from a hip collection of CDs, this is a Wild West–theme bar—sort of as if Disney had created it, but with the help of a few queens. Memorable touches include a cigar-store Indian to greet you at the front door, swinging doors, fake cacti, Navajo rugs, wagon wheels, and a bas-relief Western mural on one wall showing cowboys under a lipstick sunset. Other walls have silly photos and signs with such endearing messages as "If you ain't a cowboy you ain't shit" and "Spitting on the floors and walls is prohibited." If all this doesn't get you excited, check out the drink specials: This may be the easiest place in town to get tanked for under $5. ✉ *1723 Polk St., ☎ 415/776–4162. Crowd: 80/20 m/f, mostly thirtysomething, fun-loving, rowdy.*

The Giraffe. This is the most underrated bar in San Francisco, which means, unfortunately, that it can be pretty quiet some nights. On lower Polk Street near all the sleaze, it draws a nice (but still kind of cruisy) guy-next-door crowd. Bits of giraffe paraphernalia are strewn about, including the odd photo and statue. The cute, outgoing bartenders wear white Oxford shirts with snazzy ties. ✉ *1131 Polk St., ☎ 415/474–1702. Crowd: 80/20 m/f, mostly 20s and 30s, mix of working-class and white-collar, slightly rough but congenial.*

N' Touch. A sleek disco where Polk Street begins to get nicer is the hangout of choice for gay Asian men. The narrow bar up front can get claustrophobic on busy nights. The compact dance floor in the back has excel¹ent music; on Thursdays strippers perform before a packed house. For such a small place, this is a very hot disco. Fun for everybody, but especially enjoyable if the words *Pacific Rim* excite you. ✉ *1548 Polk St.,* ☎ *415/441–8413. Crowd: mostly male, mostly Asian, young, lively, lots of disco bunnies.*

Polk Gulch. Whew! This place is scary. Rumor has it that not one but *two* men featured on *America's Most Wanted* have hung out at the ole Gulch. Nevertheless, if you want to understand the heart and soul of Polk Street over the past two decades, you should stop by. It's a simple-looking place, with tubes of neon snaking across the wall, plus several mirrors and a few TV screens. A good place to perfect your deadly glare. ✉ *1100 Polk St.,* ☎ *415/771–2022. Crowd: male, mostly 30s and 40s, rough trade, drunk, hustlers.*

QT. The QT (a.k.a. Quick Tricks) looks like a cross between Studio 54 and a ski lodge. White, pink, and chrome cubes cling to the wall above the bar, creating an almost three-dimensional effect reminiscent of a Sylvester album cover. Vertical strips of mirror and white stucco alternate on the other walls. In the back a small elevated stage hosts diverse entertainment, from experimental jazz combos to strippers (amateur contests on Tuesdays are great fun). Several TV screens show vintage music videos, and when there isn't live music, Top 40 classics are piped in. Never a dull moment. ✉ *1312 Polk St.,* ☎ *415/885–1114. Crowd: 85/15 m/f; diverse in age; bad hair, hairpieces; tourists seeking respite from their dreary hotel rooms at the nearby Leland Hotel; sloppy drunks; many hustlers and dirty old men.*

Reflections. Regulars love this run-down bar for its pool table and Keno and old video games. The dreary maroon industrial carpeting adds a certain flavor—or odor—to the place. The name is not especially reflective of either the clientele or the decor. ✉ *1160 Polk St.,* ☎ *415/771–6262. Crowd: male, local, old.*

The Swallow. The gold nameplate outside the front door is a bit much—you'd think you'd stumbled upon the Union Club or something. This is the classiest bar on Polk Street, well north of the shadier places. There's a long bar and plenty of table seating. Every night but Tuesday you can hear some of the community's best piano performers—mostly playing show tunes. ✉ *1750 Polk St.,* ☎ *415/775–4152. Crowd: 85/15 m/f, mostly 40s and up, friendly, lots of ascots and velvet blazers.*

NEIGHBORHOOD HAUNTS

If you're up for more Polk exploring, try **Kimo's** (✉ 1351 Polk St., ☎ 415/885–4535), which has a show lounge with tired drag acts; the **Motherlode** (✉ 1002 Post St., ☎ 415/928–6006), the city's main transgender club, in the Tenderloin a block east of Polk; the **P.S. Bar** (✉ 1121 Polk St., ☎ 415/885–1448), a dreary piano lounge that's all mirrors and neon, and whose patrons all seem to be named "John"; and the **Polk Rendezvous** (✉ 1303 Polk St., ☎ 415/673–7934), a creepy cocktail lounge that's a good place to rendezvous with your bookie or pimp.

Elsewhere in San Francisco

PRIME SUSPECTS

Alta Plaza. Most evenings a gaggle of lawyers and stockbrokers flocks to this oft-teased bar, usually referred to as the "Ultra Plastic." In any other town this guppie bar wouldn't seem so out of place, but San Francisco's gay community is not usually thought to be status-conscious—the sight of guys in Armani suits swarming around a mahogany bar with exotic floral arrangements is a real anomaly. If you want to see the place in full swing, come after work for happy hour. The restaurant here is quite good (*see* Eats, *above*). Alta Plaza hosts a number charity fund-raisers throughout the year. ✉ *2301 Fillmore St., Pacific Heights,* ☎ *415/922–1444. Crowd: mostly male, young, professional, lots of designer duds, sugar daddies, and even some sugar babies.*

Lion Pub. This Pacific Heights guppie bar has been in business for more than 25 years—an early-'70s gay guide chastises its patrons for being the type "who for the most part wouldn't give a Gay Liberationist the time of day; they got theirs and are not concerned about the rest." Nasty. The crowd's less effete lately, though in the past couple of years the Lion has declined a shade in popularity. It's well known for its hunky bartenders—the owner seems to handpick on the basis of brawn. Also famous is the toasty fieldstone fireplace in back. Your parents would be at home amid the clubby decor—Tiffany-style lamps and windows, faux-

Corinthian columns, and faux-marble tables. The Lion is the Alta Plaza's major competitor, but both bars draw many of the same guys. As the night progresses, it gets livelier. ⊠ *2062 Divisadero St., Pacific Heights,* ☎ *415/567–6565. Crowd: mostly male, young to middle-age guppies, more relaxed than Alta Plaza.*

Marlena's. After work Marlena's is often crowded, and outsiders are warmly welcomed. The decor is of the gay-tacky genre, heavy on the pink. The jukebox spins old pop tunes. ⊠ *488 Hayes St., Hayes Valley,* ☎ *415/864–6672. Crowd: 60/40 m/f, 30s and older, mixed racially, quite a few transgenders and TVs.*

Mint. Conversation is easy at this clean, bright bar. Regulars and tourists chat with one another, and karaoke is on just about every night of the week—San Francisco appears to be obsessed with this phenomenon. The Mint has been up-and-running and gay since World War II. What did they do here all those years before karaoke? ⊠ *1942 Market St., Civic Center,* ☎ *415/626–4726. Crowd: 75/25 m/f, all ages, some suits, laid-back, friendly, some talented singers, some untalented singers.*

NEIGHBORHOOD HAUNTS

Downtown has few (well, no) exclusively gay hangouts, but one terribly sexy and swank lounge, the **Red Room** (⊠ Commodore Hotel, 827 Sutter St., ☎ 415/346–7666), opened in 1996 and pulls in a queer-sensible crowd. As the name suggests, the decor is red: vinyl, suede, tile, silk, crushed velvet—every sensuous material you can imagine swells in vibrant hues. It raises your body temperature just to think about it. What you do here is look uninterested and interesting at the same time, ideally with one of the bar's trademark martinis in hand.

With a list of more than 350 vintages, the **Hayes and Vine** (⊠ 377 Hayes St., Hayes Valley, ☎ 415/626–5301) will tickle your inner sommelier. The mood is casual; this is a great place to unwind with friends before hitting one of Market Street's new culinary darlings.

Finocchio's (⊠ 506 Broadway, ☎ 415/982–9388), in North Beach, has been celebrated since the '30s, more among touristy straights than gays, for its revue of female impersonators. Don't come expecting a queer environment. A much better revue, also in North Beach, is the long-running **Beach Blanket Baby-**

Ion (⌧ Club Fugazi, 678 Green St., ☎ 415/421–4222), a send-up of San Francisco landmarks and idiosyncrasies that features wacky costumes and an energetic cast. North Beach's trendy celebrity (or, more accurately, celebrity-watchers) hangout, **Tosca** (⌧ 242 Columbus Ave., ☎ 415/391–1244), is a straight bar that draws many gays—how could it not with a jukebox that plays only opera selections?

A relatively new and dapper piano bar just off Market Street, **Martuni's** (⌧ 4 Valencia St., Civic Center, ☎ 415/241–0205) has live entertainment nightly. In the Haight-Ashbury, casual **Trax** (⌧ 1437 Haight St., ☎ 415/864–4213) has a good CD jukebox.

Women's Bars and Hangouts

PRIME SUSPECTS

Wild Side West. Its owners don't like to think of this as a lesbian bar, but come see for yourself: There are an awful lot of gay gals in here. The Wild Side is in Bernal Heights, not too convenient to anything. The small place has exposed brick, a pool table, chandeliers, and a stained-glass window at the end of the bar. ⌧ *424 Cortland Ave., ☎ 415/647–3099. Crowd: 75/25 f/m; mostly lesbian but lots of straight locals.*

NEIGHBORHOOD HAUNTS

The nonalcoholic **Josie's Cabaret and Juice Joint** (⌧ 3583 16th St., ☎ 415/861–7933) books male and female performers, but often showcases performances by the nation's best-known lesbian comics and music acts.

Osento Baths (⌧ 955 Valencia St., ☎ 415/282–6333), a soothing women's (nonsexual) bathhouse in the Mission, is a relaxing spot to shake off a tense day. The **Eros** (*see* Action, *below*) sex club holds lesbian nights.

ONE-NIGHTERS, MOVEABLE FETES

Club Confidential (⌧ Embassy Lounge, 600 Polk St., ☎ 415/885–0842) is an occasional dykes-dressed-as-guys party, usually packed, that presents a few cabaret performers. Very *Victor/Victoria*. Similar in its level of sophistication, **Comme Nous** (⌧ Minna, 139 8th St., ☎ 415/626–2337) is a sapphic speakeasy held on Saturday nights in a jazzy renovated space. **Faster Pussycat!** (☎ 415/561–9771) has most recently been held on Sunday, also at Minna. This lesbian party always features a live "grrrl" band, and the place usually rocks. **G-Spot** at the **End Up** (✉ 401 Harrison St., ☎ 415/337–4962) is one of the city's most glamorous parties. In early 1997, well-known DJs Zanne and Junkyard revived their hip queerclub **Junk** (✉ Stud, 399 9th St., ☎ 415/863–6623), held on the last Saturday of the month. Queers of all colors and genders groove to funk classic, punk, and alternative sounds.

Additional dyke parties happen sporadically and at various locations: **Club Q** (☎ 415/985–5241), a Mixtress Page Hodel–hosted party on the first Friday of every month at Club Townsend (✉ 177 Townsend St.); and **In Bed With Fairy Butch** (✉ Minna, 139 8th St., ☎ 415/626–2337), always the last Friday of every month, with treats that range from a lesbian dating game to performance art.

Action

Sex clubs and private parties, as well as video arcades and porn shops, are well attended and widely available in San Francisco. The favorites include **Blow Buddies** (✉ 933 Harrison St., ☎ 415/863–4323); **Eros** (✉ 2051 Market St., ☎ 415/864–3767), which also offers professional massage; and the **Night Gallery** (✉ 1365 Folsom St., ☎ 415/255–1852). **S.F. Jacks** (☎ 415/267–6999) has parties at different locations but has most recently been settling in at the **Power Exchange Mainstation** (✉ 74 Otis St., ☎ 415/487–9944), which hosts many other events.

San Francisco is a hub of sex toys, erotica, leather, and other fun stuff. **Folsom Gulch** (✉ 947 Folsom St., ☎ 415/495–6402) has a huge selection of videos and mags, and a video arcade. **A Taste of Leather** (✉ 317A 10th St., ☎ 415/252–9166) is strong on those hard-to-find bedroom necessities—riding crops, slings, slave collars, vacuum pumps, and mouth gags.

One of the most famous adult theaters in the country is the **Campus** (✉ 220 Jones St., ☎ 415/673–3384), in the heart of the Tenderloin. Tickets are on the steep side at $12, but they're good for the whole day (in-out privileges, if you'll pardon the expression). Famous porn stars perform here regularly. Several other such theaters and video arcades are in the neighborhood, including the **Tearoom Theater** (✉ 145 Eddy St., ☎ 415/885–9887) and **Nob Hill Adult Theatre** (✉ 729 Bush St., ☎ 415/781–9468).

The **Gauntlet** (✉ 2377 Market St., ☎ 415/431–3133) has been the Castro's piercing parlor of choice for more than 20 years.

SLEEPS

No matter what your price range, San Francisco is a marvelous metropolis for accommodations, with luxurious Old World–inspired lodgings on a par with New York; small hotels rivaled in charm only by those in New Orleans; and the best selection of gay-friendly B&Bs anywhere in the country. The Kimpton Group, which owns a handful of hotels in Seattle and Portland, has about a dozen intimate, smartly done accommodations in San Francisco. Several have strong gay followings, as do the diverse Joie de Vivre inns and hotels.

If you insist on being within a short walk of the Castro, you'll need to check into one of the area's guest houses. Most of the city's best gay-frequented options are downtown, close to Nob Hill and Union Square. Here, you're a 10-minute cab ride from the Castro and an even shorter ride (or a manageable walk) from the nightclubs in SoMa; you're also close to many of the city's top attractions. Keep in mind that hotel rooms in San Francisco fill up quickly in summer and during holidays—book a couple of months ahead whenever possible. Many smaller properties share a toll-free number (☎ 800/738–7477) in high season and for occasional promotions; you can sometimes find a discount rate this way.

For price ranges, *see* the lodging chart at the front of this guide.

Hotels

Downtown Vicinity

$$$$ 🏨 **The Clift.** A Four Seasons property for many years, the luxurious Clift is now part of the Grand Heritage Hotel chain, the transition having done nothing to damage a sterling reputation. The hotel, convenient to the city's theater district, has earned the respect of the gay community with its support of AIDS and cancer charities. ✉ *495 Geary St., 94102,*

☎ *415/775–4700 or 800/652–5438,* ℻ *415/441–4621. 329 rooms. Restaurant, exercise room.*

$$$$ ▥ **Mandarin Oriental.** All the rooms have sensational views in this hotel on the top 11 floors (38–48) of San Francisco's third-tallest building. Even from your tub, a massive plate-glass window allows you to watch the fog lift above the Golden Gate Bridge. Understated Asian colors and furnishings adorn the rooms, which though luxurious are not as ornate as those in the more traditional properties on Nob Hill. ✉ *222 Sansome St., 94104,* ☎ *415/885–0999 or 800/622–0404,* ℻ *415/433–0289. 158 rooms. Restaurant.*

$$$$ ▥ **Ritz-Carlton.** Not just your ordinary Ritz-Carlton, the San Francisco property is one of the top two or three urban hotels in America. Guests inside this gorgeous neoclassic 1920 building enjoy an immense fitness center, two outstanding restaurants, and the Ritz bar, which has the country's largest collection of single-malt whiskeys. Rooms are large and luxuriously appointed with marble baths, double sinks, and vanity mirrors. ✉ *600 Stockton St., 94108,* ☎ *415/296–7465 or 800/241–3333,* ℻ *415/291–0288. 336 rooms. Restaurant, pool, health club.*

$$$–   ▥ **Campton Place.** Renowned for its personal service and
$$$$ classy but very small rooms, this exclusive hotel lies a short walking distance from SoMa nightlife. The Campton Place restaurant, which serves fantastic New American cuisine, is one of the city's best hotel restaurants. ✉ *340 Stockton St., 94108,* ☎ *415/781–5555 or 800/426–3135,* ℻ *415/955– 5536. 117 rooms. Restaurant.*

$$$–   ▥ **Huntington Hotel.** This Nob Hill hotel is less famous than
$$$$ its neighbors, but it remains one of the top three or four places to stay in San Francisco. The discreet staff aims to please but also respects your privacy. Large elegant rooms reflect a variety of decorating styles. A great hotel, from top to bottom. ✉ *1075 California St., 94108,* ☎ *415/474–5400 or 800/227– 4683,* ℻ *415/474–6227. 140 rooms. Restaurant.*

$$$–   ▥ **Hyatt Regency.** From the outside this concrete tower ap-
$$$$ pears a bit stark, but inside are stylish rooms and one of the Hyatt's trademark spectacular atriums (featured in the disaster classic *The Towering Inferno*). Atop this reliable property, which has long been a friend to the gay community, is a groovy revolving restaurant and bar. ✉ *5 Embarcadero Center, 94111,* ☎ *415/788–1234 or 800/233–1234,* ℻ *415/398– 2567. 803 rooms. 2 restaurants.*

$$$– 🏨 **Renaissance Stanford Court.** The spacious rooms in this
$$$$ former apartment building on the eastern slope of Nob Hill
have all sorts of novel creature comforts—doesn't every trav-
eler yearn for a heated towel rack? The on-site Fournou's
Ovens is one of the San Francisco's top Italian restaurants.
✉ *905 California St., 94108,* ☎ *415/989–3500 or 800/227–
4736,* ℻ *415/391–0513. 402 rooms. Restaurant, exercise
room.*

$$–$$$$ 🏨 **Fairmont.** The majestic Fairmont, whose exterior and
penthouse suite were featured on the TV series *Hotel,* is still
one of the most impressive hotels in America—from the outside. Rooms, especially in the newer wing, have lost much
of their luster (a several-year makeover is in progress), but
have beautiful views of the skyline and bay. ✉ *950 Mason
St., 94108,* ☎ *415/772–5000 or 800/527–4727,* ℻ *415/
772–5013. 597 rooms. 5 restaurants, health club.*

$$–$$$$ 🏨 **Hotel Rex.** The Joie de Vivre hotel chain's latest venture
adds a touch of Roaring Twenties style to Union Square
with murals and portraits depicting sophisticated salon so-
ciety. There's even an antiquarian bookstore on the premises.
Rooms continue this theme but also have such business
amenities as voice mail and computer data ports. Evening wine
is served in a marvelously sedate room behind the reception
desk. ✉ *562 Sutter St., 94102,* ☎ *415/433–4434 or 800/433–
4434,* ℻ *415/433–3695. 94 rooms.*

$$$ 🏨 **Hotel Monaco.** The whimsical Monaco's distinctly Parisian
flair has made the young hotel the talk of the city. The lobby,
with its soaring vaulted ceilings, trompe l'oeil murals, and
sweeping staircase, is magnificent. Rooms are no less capti-
vating, with faux-bamboo writing desks, high-back chairs,
four-poster beds, and wallpaper striped in bold colors. Many
suites have Jacuzzi tubs. The hotel's Grand Cafe is a com-
petent and stylish purveyor of California cuisine. ✉ *501
Geary St., 94102,* ☎ *415/292–0100 or 800/214–4220,* ℻
415/292–0111. 201 rooms. Restaurant, health club.

$$$ 🏨 **Prescott.** The first-rate staff puts this hotel high above the
others in the theater district. Guests staying on the concierge
level are treated to an evening reception of drinks and pizza
from Wolfgang Puck's Postrio restaurant downstairs. Some-
what small rooms are outfitted with sharp cherry-wood fur-
niture and silk wallpaper. ✉ *545 Post St., 94102,* ☎ *415/
563–0303 or 800/283–7322,* ℻ *415/563–6831. 165 rooms.
Restaurant.*

$$$ 🏨 **Tuscan Inn.** Fisherman's Wharf is without question the city's least homo-hospitable tourist district, and most of its hotels are of the bland chain variety and cater largely to families. The Tuscan is the one diamond in the rough, and it's quite accommodating to queerfolk. The contemporary redbrick exterior conceals an intimate hotel whose guest rooms are graced with white pine furniture. ⊠ *425 North Point St., 94133,* ☎ *415/561–1100 or 800/648–4626,* 🖷 *415/561–1199. 220 rooms. Restaurant.*

$$–$$$ 🏨 **Hotel Diva.** Artists and designers favor this postindustrial Theater Row hotel with a weathered chrome facade. Starkly furnished rooms are decorated in black and silver. ⊠ *440 Geary St., 94102,* ☎ *415/885–0200 or 800/553–1900,* 🖷 *415/346–6613. 107 rooms. Restaurant, exercise room.*

$$–$$$ 🏨 **Hotel Triton.** Among the Kimpton Group properties the Triton is the one that might as well have a pink-triangle welcome mat outside the front door—it markets very openly to the gay and lesbian community. The avant-garde rooms recall the Manhattan's Royalton. The seven suites were each decorated by a different celeb designer, from Joe Boxer to Suzan Briganti. Very cool. ⊠ *342 Grant Ave., 94108,* ☎ *415/394–0500 or 800/433–6611,* 🖷 *415/394–0555. 140 rooms. Restaurant, exercise room.*

$$–$$$ 🏨 **Sir Francis Drake.** Rooms at this late-1920s boutique hotel a block from Union Square are decorated with early-California furniture. The doormen look somewhat silly in their garish beefeater costumes—you'll be tempted to tease them. The dramatic high-ceilinged lobby is a striking place to meet friends before heading into Scala's for dinner or a drink (*see* Eats, *above*). ⊠ *450 Powell St., 94102,* ☎ *415/392–7755 or 800/227–5480,* 🖷 *415/391–8719. 417 rooms. 2 restaurants.*

$$–$$$ 🏨 **Vintage Court.** This romantic reasonably priced hotel has the atmosphere of a Wine Country inn, and it's among the more queer-friendly downtown properties. Complimentary wine is served each evening in the stately lobby. Even if you don't stay here, you'll want to try Masa's—the city's best French restaurant. ⊠ *650 Bush St., 94108,* ☎ *415/392–4666 or 800/654–1100,* 🖷 *415/433–4065. 107 rooms. Restaurant.*

$$–$$$ 🏨 **York Hotel.** Popular with gays, Europeans, and corporate types (in some cases all three), the York, a dour-looking gray-stone property (it was the Empire Hotel in Alfred Hitchcock's *Vertigo*), has rooms decorated with Mediterranean-inspired colors and furnishings. On the ground floor is the

Plush Room cabaret. ⊠ *940 Sutter St., 94109,* ☎ *415/885–6800 or 800/808–9675,* FAX *415/885–2115. 96 rooms. Exercise room.*

$–$$ ⊞ **Commodore International Hotel.** You won't find better accommodations at these rates so close to Union Square. What the Commodore lacks in elegance it makes up for with hip '40s-style furnishings, spacious rooms, walk-in closets, and an exceedingly artsy but playful personality. Trendoids gather nightly in the Red Room bar (*see* Scenes, *above*) and daily at the Titanic Cafe (*see* Eats, *above*). ⊠ *825 Sutter St., 94109,* ☎ *415/923–6800 or 800/338–6848,* FAX *415/923–6804. 113 rooms. Restaurant.*

$ ⊞ **Mosser Victorian Hotel.** This 1913 hotel, one of the best bargains downtown—actually, just south of Market Street, a short walk from SoMa nightlife—has clean and cheerful rooms furnished with Victorian reproductions. ⊠ *54 4th St., 94103,* ☎ *415/986–4400 or 800/227–3804,* FAX *415/495–7653. 166 rooms, some share bath. Restaurant.*

West of Downtown

$$$ ⊞ **Hotel Majestic.** A typical room inside this Edwardian palace, one of the most glamorous hotels west of Van Ness Avenue, has a fireplace, a four-poster bed, and French Empire and 19th-century English antiques. ⊠ *1500 Sutter St., 94109,* ☎ *415/441–1100 or 800/869–8966,* FAX *415/673–7331. 57 rooms. Restaurant.*

$–$$ ⊞ **The Abigail.** The Joie de Vivre chain's most conventional establishment is an inexpensive Victorian-style hotel with small modest rooms brightened by down comforters and turn-of-the-century lithographs and paintings. Midway between the Castro and downtown, it has a terrific vegetarian restaurant, the Millennium (*see* Eats, *above*), on the ground floor. ⊠ *246 McAllister St., 94102,* ☎ *415/861–9728 or 800/243–6510,* FAX *415/861–5848. 60 rooms. Restaurant.*

$–$$ ⊞ **Atherton Hotel.** This moderately priced choice on the edge of the Tenderloin has a dramatic Mediterranean-inspired lobby with etched glass, marble floors, and carved wood. Guest rooms are simple and small but quite comfortable. The Abbey Bar is fashioned out of pieces from an authentic British abbey. ⊠ *685 Ellis St., 94109,* ☎ *415/474–5720 or 800/474–5720,* FAX *415/474–8256. 75 rooms. Restaurant.*

$–$$ ⊞ **Holiday Lodge.** From the outside this Joie de Vivre–operated hostelry looks like any other motel, but rooms here are the model of cleanliness—plus they have kitchenettes and in-room laundry facilities. Beds are against mirrored walls, creating the illusion that you've got company. ⊠ *1901 Van Ness Ave., 94109,* ☎ *415/776–4469 or 800/367–8504,* 𝖥𝖠𝖷 *415/474–7046. 77 rooms. Pool.*

$–$$ 🛏 **Phoenix Inn.** This cult favorite bills itself as the city's "creative crossroads." It's also the gateway to the Tenderloin, but don't hold that against it. The fabulous Phoenix has hosted many trendy celebrities, including John Waters (alive, gay), River Phoenix (deceased, gay icon), Keith Haring (deceased, gay), Faye Dunaway (alive, gay icon), and Keanu Reeves (no comment). This '50s motor lodge had become seedy until hotelier Chip Conley converted it into a chic but still affordable lodging, famous for its pool parties and the more than 250 works of art hanging throughout the property. Be sure to check out the lively Caribbean restaurant, Miss Pearl's Jam House. ⊠ *601 Eddy St., 94109,* ☎ *415/776–1380 or 800/248–9466,* 𝖥𝖠𝖷 *415/885–3109. 44 rooms. Restaurant, pool.*

$ 🛏 **Leland Hotel.** The Leland has a sketchy reputation—it's a base for many of the neighborhood's young, eager self-starters. Nevertheless, if you're in a pinch, the rooms are clean and the staff polite. ⊠ *315 Polk St., 94109,* ☎ *415/441–5141 or 800/258–4458,* 𝖥𝖠𝖷 *415/441–1449. 104 rooms.*

$ 🛏 **Travelodge.** This chain motel is close to Polk Street and a short bus ride, or a long walk, from the Castro. ⊠ *1707 Market St., 94103,* ☎ *415/621–6775 or 800/578–7878,* 𝖥𝖠𝖷 *415/621–4305. 84 rooms.*

The Castro

$–$$ 🛏 **Beck's Motor Lodge.** This functional '60s motor lodge is a dull but cheap budget option in the Castro. ⊠ *2222 Market St., 94114,* ☎ *415/621–8212,* 𝖥𝖠𝖷 *415/241–0435. 57 rooms.*

$ 🛏 **Twin Peaks.** If you don't mind bare-bones musty accommodations, the Twin Peaks offers great daily and weekly rates. It has a good location, a block from Castro Street. ⊠ *2160 Market St., 94114,* ☎ *415/621–9467. 60 rooms.*

Guest Houses and Small Hotels

The Castro and Mission

$$–$$$ 🛏 **Inn on Castro.** This refurbished 1896 house is easily the nicest, though costliest, accommodation in the Castro. The light and airy rooms have a kitschy '50s feel about them. ⊠ *321 Castro St., 94114,* ☎ *415/861–0321. 8 rooms with phone, bath. Full breakfast. Mixed gay male/lesbian.*

$$–$$$ ⊞ **Inn San Francisco.** Feather beds and 19th-century antiques grace the rooms of this pink Italianate Victorian in Mission Hill. You'll find a sunny patio on the roof, and out back a lush garden with a redwood hot tub. ⊠ *943 S. Van Ness Ave., 94110,* ☎ *415/641–0188 or 800/359–0913,* FAX *415/641–1701. 22 rooms with phone and TV, most with private bath. Full breakfast. Mixed gay/straight.*

$$ **Black Stallion.** This is a leather-and-Levi's-themed guest house, but don't assume that all the rooms are painted black and have beer stains on the floors (as most leather bars do). Everything here is clean and bright, and if this is your scene, you'll love the friendly owners and patrons. ⊠ *635 Castro St., 94114,* ☎ *415/863–0131. 8 rooms share baths. Mostly gay male.*

$–$$ ⊞ **Castillo Inn.** This is one of the Castro's more modest, homey options. Guests have use of refrigerators and microwaves, and a new two-bedroom suite was recently added; it has a full kitchen, deck, and balcony. ⊠ *48 Henry St., 94114,* ☎ *415/864–5111 or 800/865–5112,* FAX *415/641–1321. 4 rooms with phone, TV, and shared baths. Mostly gay male.*

$–$$ ⊞ **House O'Chicks.** What's not to love about the sprightly House O'Chicks, a century-old Victorian whose rooms have VCRs (note the owners' hot collection of "chicks" porn) and CD players. This is a good place to celebrate your anniversary. ⊠ *15th St. near Noe St. (call for details), 94114,* ☎ *415/861–9849. 3 rooms with phone and TV, 1 with private bath. Lesbian.*

$ ⊞ **Dolores Park Inn.** Not everybody adores the gritty feel of the Mission District, at least as a place to stay, but a visit to the Dolores Park Inn may change your outlook. Antiques fill this 1874 Italianate Victorian, and there's a garden in the back. Good breakfast, too. ⊠ *3641 17th St., 94114,* ☎ FAX *415/621–0482 or 415/861–9335. 4 rooms with phone, TV, and shared baths; carriage house. Continental breakfast. No credit cards. Mixed gay/straight.*

$ **24 Henry Street.** This centrally located B&B is bright and cozy, and the two gents who operate it will gladly dispense tips about the Castro and the city. The suites here hold three people and have kitchens. ⊠ *24 Henry St., 94114,* ☎ *415/864–5686 or 800/900–5686,* FAX *415/864–0406. 10 rooms, some with TV, private bath. Mostly gay male.*

East of Van Ness Avenue

$$$–
$$$$ ⌦ **Nob Hill Lambourne.** Women executives often choose the sumptuous Lambourne, a cross between an urban spa and a state-of-the-art business center. Guests have access to personal computers and laser printers, but can also partake of an herbal wrap in the on-site spa. Rooms have contemporary furnishings and kitchenettes. You'll receive the most personal attention here of any downtown hotel. ⊠ *725 Pine St., 94108,* ☎ *415/433–2287 or 800/274–8466,* ℻ *415/433–0975. 20 rooms with TV, phone, and private bath. Continental breakfast. Mixed gay/straight.*

$$–$$$ ⌦ **Hotel La Bohème.** In otherwise straight North Beach you may be surprised to find a property with several gay employees. Even better, this charmer with a great location amid the trattorias and coffeehouses along Columbus Avenue has attractively furnished rooms. The staff is highly professional and attentive. ⊠ *444 Columbus Ave., 94133,* ☎ *415/433–9111,* ℻ *415/362–6292. 15 rooms with phone, TV, and private bath. Mostly straight.*

$ ⌦ **Pensione International Hotel.** This is one of San Francisco's most affordable options, especially if you're willing to forgo a private bath. It's surprisingly cheerful for a budget choice, and breakfast is included. ⊠ *875 Post St., 94109,* ☎ *415/775–3344. 46 rooms with phone and TV, all share baths. Mixed gay/straight.*

West of Van Ness Avenue

$$$–
$$$$ ⌦ **Anna's Three Bears.** The three over-the-top suites in this 1906 gray-and-white inn have fully stocked kitchens, Edwardian antiques, fireplaces, and private decks. This Buena Vista Heights hostelry is especially nice for a longer stay. If you factor in the self-catering option, the weekly rates of $1,000 to $1,400 can be bargains. ⊠ *114 Divisadero St., 94117,* ☎ *415/255–3167 or 800/428–8559,* ℻ *415/552–2959. 3 rooms with phone, TV, and private bath. Continental breakfast. Mixed gay/straight.*

$$–$$$$ ⌦ **Archbishops Mansion.** A backdrop for many gay weddings, this Second Empire–style inn, built in 1904 for the city's Catholic archbishop, is one of the most romantic properties in California. Rooms are enormous and filled with Belle Epoque furnishings; many have separate sitting areas and fireplaces. They're each quite special, too; the Don Giovanni suite has a seven-head shower, which should appeal to any guest with an especially clean (or the opposite) imagination. ⊠ *1000*

Fulton St., 94117, ☎ *415/563–7872 or 800/543–5820,* FAX *415/885–3193. 15 rooms with phone, TV, and private bath. Continental breakfast. Mixed gay/straight.*

$$–$$$$ 🏨 **Chateau Tivoli.** Rodney Karr and Willard Gersbach run this ornate 1892 Victorian, which glows with 22 vibrant colors. If you're impressed by the fanciful exterior, check out the elaborate rooms, decked top to bottom with antiques and collectibles (including a few too many stuffed and mounted animals). It's difficult to walk through this museumlike mansion without humming the opening bars to the *Addams Family* theme song. ☒ *1057 Steiner St., 94115,* ☎ *415/776–5462 or 800/228–1647,* FAX *415/776–0505. 7 rooms with phone, most with private bath. Continental breakfast (full on weekends). Mixed gay/straight.*

$$–$$$$ 🏨 **The Mansions.** A pair of excessively ornate Queen Anne Victorians in Pacific Heights, the Mansions complex is as entertaining as it is functional. Curios and art objects abound, and each room features a striking mural of the famous person for which it is named. Barbra Streisand once stayed in the Louis IV room, but so far there don't seem to be any plans to rename it after her. Every night owner Bob Pritikin presents a live magic show; supposedly a ghost haunts the premises. ☒ *2220 Sacramento St., 94115,* ☎ *415/929–9444 or 800/826–9398,* FAX *415/567–9391. 21 rooms with phone and private bath. Restaurant. Mixed gay/straight.*

$$–$$$ 🏨 **Albion House Inn.** This courtly old inn close to Hayes Valley's great restaurants has vintage wallpaper and art and many antiques and collectibles. ☒ *135 Gough St., 94102,* ☎ *415/ 621–0896 or 800/625–2466,* FAX *415/621–3811. 8 rooms with phone and private bath. Full breakfast. Mixed gay/straight.*

$$–$$$ 🏨 **Queen Anne Hotel.** A four-story former girls boarding school built in 1890 houses this top-notch hotel with an extremely helpful staff. Each of the 48 rooms is furnished differently, with a mix of new and antique pieces; many have fireplaces and wet bars. ☒ *1590 Sutter St., 94109,* ☎ *415/ 441–2828 or 800/227–3970,* FAX *415/775–5212. 48 rooms with phone, TV, and private bath. Continental breakfast. Mixed gay/straight.*

$–$$ 🏨 **Bock's B&B.** If you don't mind staying in the suburban-feeling Inner Sunset, this woman-owned Edwardian home with period-style furnishings is an inexpensive option. The house has decks with great city views. (Nonsmokers only; two-night

minimum.) ⊠ *1448 Willard St., 94117,* ☏ *415/664–6842.*
3 rooms with phone and TV, 2 share a bath. Continental
breakfast. Mixed gay/straight.

$–$$ 🏨 **Red Victorian.** This is one of the strangest properties in
town, a true theme hotel. The Summer of Love room has a
tie-dyed canopy bed; other accommodations have similarly
quirky decorating schemes and touches. The place may bring
back memories of bad acid trips, but it's clean and run by a
pleasant bunch. ⊠ *1665 Haight St., 94117,* ☏ *415/864–1978,*
415/863–3293. 18 rooms with phone and private bath.
Continental breakfast. Mostly straight.

$ 🏨 **Carl Street Unicorn House.** This small guest house near
Buena Vista Park is a safe place for women. The two rooms
share one bath, but that's the only drawback. The beautiful
1895 house is filled with owner Miriam Weber's many collectibles. ⊠ *156 Carl St., 94117,* ☏ *415/753–5194. 2 rooms*
share a bath. Continental breakfast. Mostly women; mixed
lesbian/straight.

$ 🏨 **Metro Hotel.** Not too far from the Castro and about a 10-
minute walk north to the edge of the Haight, the Metro is
distinctive for its pink neon sign and funky crowd. Rooms
are large and pleasant. ⊠ *319 Divisadero St., 94117,* ☏ *415/*
861–5364. 23 rooms with phone, TV, and private bath.
Restaurant. Mixed gay/straight.

THE LITTLE BLACK BOOK

At Your Fingertips

AIDS Hotline (☏ 415/863–2437). **Community United Against
Violence Hotline (CUAV)** (☏ 415/333–4357). **Deaf Gay and
Lesbian Center** (☏ 415/255–9944, TTY 415/255–9797). **Gay
and Lesbian Helpline** (☏ 415/772–4357). **Lavender Youth
Recreation Information Center** (⊠ 127 Collingwood St., ☏
415/703–6150). **Lyon-Martin Women's Health Services** (☏
415/565–7667). **San Francisco Convention and Visitors Bureau** (⊠ 201 3rd St., Suite 900, 94103, ☏ 415/974–6900).
**San Francisco Gay/Lesbian/Bisexual/Transgender Commu-
nity Center Project** (☏ 415/864–3733). **"What's Up" Hotline
for African-American Lesbians** (☏ 510/835–6126). **Women's
Building** (⊠ 3543 18th St., ☏ 415/431–1180).

Gay Media

The two most widely read gay newspapers are the weekly
Bay Area Reporter (☏ 415/861–5019) and the biweekly *San*

Francisco Bay Times (☎ 415/227–0800). The monthly newspaper *Icon* (☎ 415/282–0942) serves as the best resource for lesbians. The biweekly *Frontiers San Francisco* (☎ 415/487–6000) runs entertainment and feature stories. *Odyssey* (☎ 415/621–6514) is a handy biweekly fag rag with detailed boys' and girls' club information and lots of fun dish. *Q San Francisco* (☎ 800/999–9718), a flashy bimonthly gay news and entertainment magazine, provides excellent bar, restaurant, and arts coverage. The monthly *Oblivion* (☎ 415/487–5498) has good bar and sex-club info, plus some community coverage. Both the *Bay Guardian* (☎ 415/255–3100) and the *San Francisco Weekly* (☎ 415/541–0700) are free alternative papers with performing-arts listings and left-of-center political commentary.

BOOKSTORES

A Different Light Bookstore (✉ 489 Castro St., ☎ 415/431–0891), the city's major lesbigay bookstore, is the city's unofficial gay welcoming center. **Books Inc.** (✉ 2275 Market St., ☎ 415/864–6777) is an excellent general independent bookstore in the Castro with a strong lesbigay section. **Modern Times** (✉ 888 Valencia St., ☎ 415/282–9246) in the Mission carries many left-leaning titles and queer-studies texts. **Bernal Books** (✉ Cortland Ave., ☎ 415/550–0293) is a neighborhood store in Bernal Heights with a sizable lesbigay section. The Civic Center's **A Clean Well-Lighted Place For Books** (✉ 601 Van Ness Ave., ☎ 415/567–6876) has an excellent lesbigay section and is strong on cookbooks and the performing and fine arts.

City Lights Bookstore (✉ 261 Columbus Ave., ☎ 415/362–8193) has long been associated with the Beat Generation. **McDonald's Book Shop** (✉ 48 Turk St., ☎ 415/673–2235) is a crazy, haphazard place with enough stacks of books and piles of magazines to keep you browsing for days.

Working Out

Gay gyms are easy to find all around town. Some of the most popular include the cruisy **City Athletic Club** (✉ 2500 Market St., ☎ 415/552–6680); **Gold's Gym** (✉ 333 Valencia St., ☎ 415/626–8865) in the Mission; the **Muscle System** (✉ 364 Hayes St., ☎ 415/863–4701; ✉ 2275 Market St., ☎ 415/863–4700), a.k.a. "the Muscle Sisters," whose two locations draw buff boys; the coed **Market Street Gym** (✉ 2301 Market St.,

☎ 415/626–4488), one of the most crowded and gayest gyms in the city; the snazzy **Pacific Heights Health Club** (✉ 2356 Pine St., ☎ 415/563–6694), with separate facilities for men and women; **Purely Physical Fitness** (✉ 1414 Castro St., ☎ 415/282–1329), nice if you're not into a big scene; and the **Women's Training Center** (✉ 2164 Market St., ☎ 415/864–6835), a smaller gym patronized by dykes and straight women that offers personal training and helpful service.

2 *Out in* the Bay Area

FEW CITIES IN THE WORLD offer more breathtaking nearby excursions than San Francisco. Within an hour's drive you'll find redwood groves, beaches, and wildlife preserves. Marin County, the least populous of San Francisco's neighboring counties, is also the most rugged and beautiful. The East Bay cities of Oakland and Berkeley have substantial lesbian and visible gay-male populations. The Peninsula is a mix of bedroom communities, small cities, remote mountains, and Pacific beaches. Because the entire region lends itself to day trips from San Francisco, lodging options are not included except for the seaside town of Half Moon Bay.

THE LAY OF THE LAND

Marin County

Hilly Marin County holds some of the Bay Area's most eye-popping scenery. Marin isn't particularly queer, though the small town of San Anselmo has a lesbigay community center (*see* The Little Black Book, *below*). There may not be a wealthier county in America with a more progressive outlook, perhaps owing to a hippie infiltration in the 1960s. Many of these radicals and former commune dwellers, some of whom were gay, are now, ironically, among the landed gentry.

Drive or bike across the Golden Gate Bridge, take your first exit (Alexander Avenue) from U.S. 101, and head through the tunnel under the highway and up steep, windy **Conzelman Road** into the **Marin Headlands.** You'll be rewarded with views back toward San Francisco. This road and Bunker Road wind through the former military installations that are now part of the **Golden Gate National Recreation Area.** A visitor

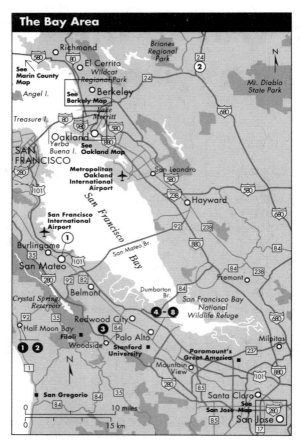

The Bay Area

Eats ●

Andalé
Taqueria, **5**

Good Earth, **7**

Pasta Moon, **1**

Printer's
Inc., **4**

Stars Palo
Alto, **6**

Sushi Ya, **8**

2 Fools
Market and
Cafe, **2**

Village Pub, **3**

Scenes ○

B Street, **1**

J.R.'s, **2**

center (✉ Field and Bunker Rds., ☎ 415/331–1540) has maps and information.

Northeast of the Golden Gate Bridge are Sausalito and Tiburon, two breezy towns with sea-level views of San Francisco. Most of the shops and restaurants in touristy **Sausalito** are along **Bridgeway,** a busy road that skirts the waterfront. An esplanade runs along much of it, past the many houseboats and pleasure craft docked just offshore in Richardson Bay. The area once housed numerous brothels and saloons that provided amusement to the shipyard workers who labored here until as recently as four decades ago. One of the old warehouses has been converted into **Village Fair** (✉ 777 Bridgeway, ☎ 415/332–2834), a complex of cutesy shops and crafts boutiques. Expensive homes crowd the hills above Sausalito, one of the straightest-feeling Bay Area communities.

Considerably less frenetic **Tiburon** sits across Richardson Bay from Sausalito, east off U.S. 101 via Tiburon Boulevard (Highway 131). Tiburon's waterfront stares across Raccoon Strait at Angel Island, and beyond that the San Francisco skyline. On a nice day, skip the drive across the bridge and take the **Red and White Fleet** (☎ 415/546–2628) ferry from Pier 43½ at Fisherman's Wharf to Tiburon and Angel Island. Check out the restaurants that line Tiburon's **Main Street,** find one with an expansive deck overlooking the bay, and dine and relax. Bikers and hikers can head over to **Angel Island.** You can rent bikes by the island's ferry terminal and pick up maps and information at the visitor center.

Mill Valley is an upscale community with more shops and restaurants. Most are downtown around **Lytton Square,** at the corner of Miller and Throckmorton avenues. If you're coming from San Francisco on U.S. 101, take the Mill Valley/Stinson Beach exit (Highway 1) and head right onto Almonte Boulevard at the stoplight where Highway 1 heads west to the ocean. Almonte Boulevard eventually becomes Miller Avenue.

The lesbian poet Elsa Gidlow, whose 1920s volume *On a Grey Thread* referred openly to same-sex love, settled in Mill Valley in the 1950s and hosted a number of like-minded artists and free thinkers.

Sixty-three-hundred-acre **Mt. Tamalpais State Park** (☎ 415/388–2070) has about 50 miles of trails for hikers of all

abilities. The ranger station is at Panoramic Highway's intersection with Pan Toll Road. Some of the redwoods in **Muir
Woods National Monument** (⌧ Muir Woods Rd., off Panoramic
Hwy., ☎ 415/388–2595), a 550-acre trail-laced grove, are
nearly 1,000 years old. Even if you haven't hiked much or only
have a couple of hours, it's possible to get a feel for these two
special parks. One caveat: Parking near the trailheads can be
difficult, especially on warm weekends. Consider arriving either before 10 AM or after 4 PM to avoid congestion.

Heading up the Marin County coast on Highway 1 you'll
pass through the sparsely populated communities of **Muir
Beach** and **Stinson Beach.** The latter has a few restaurants,
several motels, and a 3-mile beach that's great for surfing and
sunning. Continuing north above Stinson Beach, just after
Highway 1 passes by the lagoon, a left turn onto Olema–Bolinas Road leads into the hippie village of **Bolinas.** This community's residents have made such a big fuss of removing the
signs directing visitors to town that just about everybody heading up Highway 1 now makes it a side trip—so much for that
idea. Bolinas is a liberal and homo-hospitable place; same-
sexers will feel more at home at its handful of inexpensive
eateries than at the yuppified and crowded restaurants in
Tiburon and Sausalito. But don't come with high expecta-
tions; this is a sleepy part of the world.

Back on Highway 1 it's a short drive north to the town of
Inverness and the visitor center of the **Point Reyes National
Seashore** (⌧ Bear Valley Rd., ☎ 415/663–1092). Its highly
informative museum has exhibits describing the 110-square-
mile park's trails and ecology. From the visitor center, a 40-
minute drive and a challenging walk down 300 cliff-hugging
steps lead to a historic lighthouse. With many scenic drives
and great beaches, Point Reyes, a mere hour and 15 minutes
north of San Francisco, is one of the most underrated federal parks. Little Inverness has some terrific restaurants.

The East Bay

The East Bay, anchored by the compact and hilly cities of
Berkeley and Oakland, is at once cosmopolitan and accessible. For lesbians and gays, the area—especially Berkeley—
is a tolerant and exciting place to call home. But unlike
scenic Marin, sightseeing will not keep most visitors busy for
more than a full day. Dining, nightlife, and arts opportuni-
ties are abundant, however.

An ideal way to see the East Bay is to arrive for lunch at one of north Berkeley's so-called Gourmet Ghetto restaurants. Spend the afternoon checking out the University of California–Berkeley and downtown Oakland, grab a bite at one of either city's ethnic dining spots, drop by an Oakland blues or Berkeley folk-music venue, and perhaps complete the day with a wander through the White Horse Tavern, the Bay Area's longest-running gay bar.

Berkeley

About a third of the 100,000 residents of **Berkeley** work for or attend U.C. Berkeley, whose reputation for liberal politics and radical activism dates back many years. This largely accounts for the heavy presence of lesbians (many of whom were among the pioneers of West Coast feminism) and gay men here.

Although some queer San Franciscans find Berkeley too grungy and PC, one local who's experienced both prefers Berkeley: "It's friendlier, has more open spaces, and is much more integrated—not ghettoized. Everyone says San Francisco is so international and multicultural, but each group keeps to its own neighborhood. It's not paradise over here, but in Berkeley and Oakland you see all varieties of people living, working, and playing together—my neighbors are Asian, black, Latino, white, young, old, and openly queer. And we all acknowledge each other on the street."

Life here is more mainstream than it was during the '60s, but Berkeley remains a bastion of free-spirited behavior and radical thinking.

A gay-male literary subculture, closely associated with Oakland native and early queer poet and activist Robert Duncan, thrived at U.C. Berkeley throughout the '40s. More recently the city has passed comprehensive laws embracing lesbian and gay rights. In 1984 Berkeley became the nation's first municipality to provide benefits for the domestic partners of its gay employees.

Lesbian literary icon Gertrude Stein was born and spent her early years in Oakland, though the region's feminist movement didn't take hold until the 1960s, when women's bookstores, coffeehouses, social spaces, and bars began to thrive. One of the world's most extensive lesbian archives, the June Mazer Collection, now housed in Los Angeles, was begun in the early 1980s in Berkeley. Academically, U.C. Berkeley remains a hotbed of feminist thinking, and small but prestigious all-women Mills College in Oakland is sometimes jokingly called the East Bay's "own little dyke farm."

The East Bay is currently without an exclusively lesbian bar, though women-oriented restaurants and cafés remain vibrant. Mama Bears in Oakland is one of the nation's premiere lesbian-feminist bookstores, and the city's Olivia Records, the women's record label, has diversified into a world-renowned tour and cruise operator.

Most of Berkeley's attractions revolve around the beautiful **U.C. Berkeley** campus. Its visitor center (⊠ University Hall, Room 101, University Ave. and Oxford St., ☎ 510/642–5215) offers guided and self-guided tours. The social hub is **Sproul Plaza** (⊠ Telegraph Ave., at Bancroft Way), where pamphleteers distribute fliers on the cause du jour and a motley array of buskers bangs bongos and strums guitars. The landscaped campus has many notable buildings, including the 307-foot-tall **Sather Tower** (you can take an elevator to an observation deck 175 feet up), which was modeled after the campanile in Venice's Piazza San Marco. The collection of the **University Art Museum** (⊠ 2626 Bancroft Way, ☎ 510/642–0808) consists of predominantly 20th-century modern works, including many by abstract expressionist Hans Hoffman, but spans many centuries and cultures. The museum has held several queer-oriented exhibitions in recent years.

Up on U.C. Berkeley's eastern slope, the 34-acre **Botanical Garden** (⊠ Centennial Dr. in Strawberry Canyon, ☎ 510/642–3343) has nearly 14,000 plants from all over the world. The **Lawrence Hall of Science** (⊠ Centennial Dr. near Grizzly Peak Blvd., ☎ 510/642–5132) is an imposing science-education center with exhibits, films, and presentations geared principally for children.

Student-oriented shopping and dining lies south and southwest of campus along north–south-running **Telegraph Avenue** and east–west-running **Ashby Avenue. Futura** (⊠ 2360 Telegraph Ave., ☎ 510/843–3037) is fun for retro wear and a must-visit for uniform fetishists. **Buffalo Exchange** (⊠ 2512 Telegraph Ave., ☎ 510/644–9202; in Oakland, ⊠ 3333 Lakeshore Ave., ☎ 510/452–4464) keeps dykes coming back for discarded duds. **Amoeba** (✉ 2455 Telegraph Ave., ☎ 510/549–1125) overflows with used CDs. Also on Telegraph is Berkeley's lesbian and gay community space, the **Pacific Center** (✉ 2712 Telegraph Ave., ☎ 510/841–6224).

University Avenue, which runs east–west from U.C. Berkeley's campus to the **Berkeley Marina,** offers few thrills, but is home to the 1917 **U.C. Theater** (✉ 2036 University Ave., ☎ 510/843–6267), which presents the *Rocky Horror Picture Show* late-night on Saturdays, and foreign, rep, and art films the rest of the time. If you're a film fan, also check out the **Pacific Film Archive** (✉ 2621 Durant Ave., ☎ 510/642–1124), which often has queer-themed offerings.

North of campus, Euclid Avenue, Vine Street, and Shattuck Avenue form the borders of the **Gourmet Ghetto.** Alice Waters's famed **Chez Panisse** (*see* Eats, *below*) spawned a slew of competitors and organic markets. The famous **Berkeley Bowl Marketplace** (✉ 2777 Shattuck Ave., ☎ 510/843–6929) sells amazingly fresh fish, grains, produce, and other delicious things—it's also the perfect place to exchange recipes with cute customers who happen by. The **Cheeseboard** (✉ 1504 Shattuck Ave., ☎ 510/549–3183) is ideal for baked breads, cheeses, and pizzas.

The hills above Berkeley and Oakland are dotted with impressive homes and traversed by winding roads, though several hundred structures burned during the tragic fires of 1991. It's easy to maintain your bearings since you can almost always see the bay and San Francisco in the distance.

Oakland

Oakland is one of America's forgotten cities. What began as a major 19th-century agricultural center grew into a densely settled metropolis in the early 1900s, but lost some of its luster following World War II as the suburbs expanded and industry shifted elsewhere. Downtown growth in this blue-collar city has been stunted by several regressive stabs at urban renewal, though the blocks immediately surrounding Lake Merritt remain cheerful.

With as diverse a racial and ethnic population as any in America, Oakland has a wealth of shops, restaurants, and music clubs spanning several cultures. Lesbians and gay men live in several Oakland neighborhoods, especially those close to Berkeley, but downtown, except perhaps around Jack London Square, could not be described as gay-friendly.

A narrow band of grassy lawn surrounds most of Oakland's urban anchor, 155-acre **Lake Merritt.** Along the north shore is **Lakeside Park,** the site of the **Natural Science Center and Waterfowl Refuge** (✉ Perkins St., at Bellevue Ave., ☎ 510/238–3739). Migrating birds nest here in spring and summer. Walking around Lake Merritt amid the buzz of pedestrians, one can't help but notice the city's tremendous potential— Oakland's skyline includes art deco, beaux arts, and Victorian beauties in various states of repair. Along Lake Merritt's southwest shore, you can tour a vestige of this once-posh Victorian residential neighborhood, the 1876 **Camron-Stanford House** (✉ 1418 Lakeside Dr., ☎ 510/836–1976). A couple blocks south of the lake, the **Oakland Museum of California** (✉ 1000 Oak St., ☎ 510/238–3401) contains art, documents, and exhibits tracing the state's history.

One downtown site of particular interest to film fans and architecture buffs is the restored 1931 **Paramount Theater** (✉ 2025 Broadway, ☎ 510/465–6400). This art deco stunner, the main stage of the Oakland Ballet, often screens classic Hollywood films.

West of downtown on a cul-de-sac hemmed in by I–980, 14 restored Victorian homes make up **Preservation Park** (✉ Martin Luther King Dr. at 13th St.). Except for the **White House Café,** most are closed to the public.

Telegraph Avenue leads north back toward Berkeley. Lesbians are most welcome at **Mama Bears** (*see* Gay Media *in* The Little Black Book, *below*), a women's bookshop, coffeehouse, and social center.

College Avenue from Broadway to Alcatraz Avenue runs through the heart of Oakland's Rockridge neighborhood. Gays know a good neighborhood when they see one, which is probably why so many have emigrated from San Francisco to this eminently livable quarter. Rockridge has the feel of Noe Valley but is even more relaxed. Cafés and restaurants abound; shops carry everything from tribal art to secondhand clothing to the latest Birkenstock styles.

The Peninsula

The area immediately south of San Francisco, known as the Peninsula, takes in San Mateo, Hillsborough, Burlingame, Palo Alto, Woodside, and, along the coast, Half Moon Bay. Palo Alto is one of America's straightest college towns. The other Peninsula cities are low-key bedroom communities of little interest to the visitor. The bay side of the Peninsula, especially along U.S. 101, is built up, but the area toward the ocean is more geographically varied, with narrow roads, overgrown mountains, and quirky little villages.

Note that in fall 1997, the area code for Peninsula towns between San Francisco and the lower South Bay will change from 415 to 650. The grace period when calls dialed using the old code will be put through will last until fall 1998.

Stanford University (✉ Palm Dr., off University Ave., ☎ 415/723–2053) dominates the western end of **Palo Alto.** Once California governor Leland Stanford's horse farm, Stanford's 8,200 acres of rolling fields now hold the West Coast's most prestigious institution of higher learning. Although it's not as visibly queer as some universities, Stanford does have a vocal gay contingent that brings in speakers and works on homo "quality of life" issues. Life wasn't always so pink, however. Mattachine Society founder-to-be Harry Hay attended the university back in the 1930s, but feeling oppressed and unhappy, according to one biographer he split before graduating.

The talented Frederick Law Olmsted laid out the campus core, but its red-tile-roof Romanesque sandstone buildings border on the impersonal. More impressive is the 285-foot tower rising above the school's **Hoover Institution on War, Revolution, and Peace;** there's an observation deck at the top. The **Stanford Art Gallery** (☎ 415/723–3469) beside the Hoover tower contains a mix of student works, exhibitions on university history, and temporary shows. The nearby **Stanford Museum of Art** (✉ Lomita Dr., ☎ 415/723–4177), which has been out of commission since the 1989 Loma Prieta earthquake, is scheduled to reopen in fall 1998. An outdoor sculpture garden is filled with Rodin bronzes.

You'll find ritzy shopping and beautiful homes north of campus along and around tree-lined University Avenue. Though the funk factor is very low for a college town, the quality of the stores and restaurants is uniformly high.

Should a brush with staid Palo Alto leave you yearning for a dose of retro camp, visit the 16,000-doll **Barbie Hall of Fame** (⊠ 433 Waverly St., ☎ 415/326–5841). Aspiring drag queens will want to take detailed notes.

Woodside to Half Moon Bay

Most visitors to San Francisco neglect the hills south of the city in favor of the better-known Marin Headlands, but the also-stunning lower swath can easily be toured in several hours. Half Moon Bay makes for a great seaside excursion.

A good way to tour this area is to drive south from San Francisco for about 20 minutes on I–280, exiting on Cañada Road. Follow this south as it winds beside Upper Crystal Springs Reservoir. *Dynasty* fans will immediately recognize one of the most magnificent estates in California, **Filoli** (⊠ Cañada Rd. near Edgewood Rd., Woodside, ☎ 415/364–2880). The 1916 Georgian-style mansion and its 16 acres of gardens were the exteriors for the long-running TV show's Carrington estate. Hiking trails lace the property's 620 additional acres. The house, built of Flemish bond brick, contains priceless original furnishings, and the grounds include dozens of linked formal gardens. Continue south on Cañada Road to **Woodside,** which has a handsome village center, some shops, and many beautiful homes.

In downtown Woodside turn right onto Highway 84 (La Honda Road) and follow it up through the village of La Honda—a mountaintop community of latter-day hippies and bikers—then continue down Highway 84 until it hits Highway 1. Turn right and follow this back toward San Francisco. On the way you'll pass through the town of **Half Moon Bay,** once a rural seaside village and now an increasingly touristy weekend retreat. Downtown has been spoiled to a certain extent by overbuilding, but it's still a good place to stop for a snack or to window-shop. The city's five beaches are excellent for surfing, although they're too cool and breezy most days for sunbathing.

Another way to explore the hills south of San Francisco is to exit from I–280 just before the Cañada Road exit, at Highway 35, also called Skyline Boulevard, and follow this south along the largely undeveloped mountain ridge, down through Woodside and Sky Londa. The road eventually ends at Highway 17, midway between San Jose and Santa Cruz.

In case you want to be welcomed there.

We're here to see that you're always welcomed at establish-ments everywhere. That's why millions of people carry the American Express® Card – for peace of mind, confidence, and security, around the world or just around the corner.

do more ®

In case you're running low.

We're here to help with more than 118,000 Express Cash locations around the world. In order to enroll, just call American Express before you start your vacation.

And just in case.

We're here with American Express® Travelers Cheques and Cheques *for Two*.® They're the safest way to carry money on your vacation and the surest way to get a refund, practically anywhere, anytime.
Another way we help you...

do more.

AMERICAN
EXPRESS

**Travelers
Cheques**

This drive takes a while, but you'll be rewarded with excellent views. (Skyline Boulevard begins in southwestern San Francisco at Sloat Boulevard, just above Lake Merced, but the scenery doesn't really come alive until Cañada Road.)

One of the country's oldest nude beaches, at **San Gregorio** (but not to be confused with adjacent San Gregorio State Beach), is about 8 or so miles south of Half Moon Bay, just north of Highway 1's junction with Highway 84. Park your car (there's a fee) and walk north along the beach past amicable straightfolk until Friends of Dorothy predominate. Another entrance is on Highway 1, usually marked by an orange flag (as is the southern one), about 2 miles north of Highway 84, but it's a steeper climb back to your car.

GETTING AROUND

From San Francisco there's only one way to get to Marin by car: across the Golden Gate Bridge. U.S. 101 heads north through the middle of Marin County. Take U.S. 101's Mill Valley–Stinson Beach exit to get onto coastal Highway 1. Cross the San Francisco–Oakland Bay Bridge (I–80) to get to the East Bay. Head north on I–80 for Berkeley, and east on I–580 to I–980 for Oakland. Take I–280 south to get to the Peninsula or, alternatively, the busier and less-scenic U.S. 101.

Driving to downtown Berkeley or Oakland from San Francisco takes about 25 minutes. Getting to Woodside is about the same, to Palo Alto it's 30 to 40 minutes. San Rafael is about a half hour away from the city.

Golden Gate Transit (☏ 415/923–2000) buses and ferries service Marin County. Comfy **BART** (☏ 415/992–2278) trains go to both Berkeley and Oakland, as do the less-efficient buses of **AC Transit** (☏ 510/839–2882). **SamTrans** buses and **CalTrain** (☏ 800/660–4287 for both) will get you to the Peninsula.

EATS

For price ranges, *see* the chart at the front of this guide.

Marin County

Inverness

$$ ✕ **Vladimir's.** One of a handful of businesses in the sleepy village of Inverness serves hearty Czech food—veal, pork, dumplings, and soups. If you're planning to hike through neighboring Point Reyes, this is a good spot to fill up. ✉ *Sir Francis Drake Blvd.,* ☎ *415/669–1021. No credit cards.*

Mill Valley

$$–$$$ ✕ **Buckeye Roadhouse.** This Mill Valley "roadhouse" right off U.S. 101 ain't no roadhouse, but then creator Cindy Pawlcyn also gave us San Francisco's Fog City Diner, which by most accounts ain't no diner. The Buckeye is all hunting lodge in appearance, with a massive stone fireplace and dark wood walls. The American chow is prepared exquisitely but without many nouvelle touches—just tasty pork chops, baby back ribs, and a noteworthy lemon tart for dessert. ✉ *15 Shoreline Hwy.,* ☎ *415/331–2600.*

$$–$$$ ✕ **Piazza D'Angelo.** With an atmosphere and menu that are equal parts Napa Valley and Tuscany, this smart trattoria draws the see-and-be-seen crowd every weekend. Always terrific are carpaccio with mustard, capers, and Parmesan cheese; calzones stuffed with ricotta, mozzarella, spinach, and sausage; and several house-made pastas. The pace can be frenetic, however. ✉ *22 Miller Ave.,* ☎ *415/388–2000.*

$–$$ ✕ **Jennie Low's.** Cookbook writer and doyenne of traditional Chinese cooking Jennie Low presents a broad range of cuisines—spicy eggplant, crisp green beans in a piquant garlic sauce, and Hunan prawns are all winners. Busy and somewhat noisy. ✉ *38 Miller Ave.,* ☎ *415/388–8868.*

Point Reyes Station

$$ ✕ **Station House Cafe.** It's never attained star status, but this casual New American restaurant near the Point Reyes National Seashore is outstanding. Barbecued oysters are a specialty, but anything from the sea is guaranteed to be fresh and deftly prepared. Try to get a seat in the serene (if often breezy) lattice-covered garden. ✉ *11180 Hwy. 1,* ☎ *415/663–1515.*

Sausalito

$$–$$$ ✕ **Sushi Ran.** Skip the touristy and overpriced seafood houses along Bridgeway and partake of some of the Bay Area's finest sushi. The saki selection is tremendous. ✉ *107 Caledonia St.,* ☎ *415/332–3620.*

Marin County

Eats ●

Buckeye Roadhouse, **6**

Depot Bookstore and Cafe, **3**

Guaymas, **7**

Jennie Low's, **5**

Old Sam's Anchor Cafe, **8**

Piazza D'Angelo, **4**

Station House Cafe, **2**

Sushi Ran, **9**

Vladimir's, **1**

Scenes ○

Aunt Ruby's, **1**

Tiburon

$$–$$$ ✕ **Guaymas.** Favorites at this polished (though a tad pricey) regional Mexican restaurant include roasted duck in a pumpkin seed sauce and a rich chicken mole. The views from the deck are the real treat. ⊠ *5 Main St.,* ☎ *415/435–6300.*

$–$$ ✕ **Old Sam's Anchor Café.** On the sunniest afternoon of your visit to San Francisco, consider driving over to Tiburon for a dockside meal overlooking the bay and the distant city skyline. The food should hardly matter at this point, but Sam's has good sandwiches, salads, and omelets (one with oysters, bacon, and cheese). ⊠ *27 Main St.,* ☎ *415/435–4527.*

East Bay

Berkeley

$$$–$$$$ ✕ **Chez Panisse Café.** The turf of Alice Waters, the legendary pioneer of New American cooking, is worth the trip over the Bay Bridge—if you've called ahead for a reservation. The Martha Stewart–esque dining room is almost too perfect, but the food is wonderful, including such unusual creations as roast truffled breast of hen. You can also dine in the upstairs café on cheaper, more familiar, but no less creative fare. ⊠ *1517 Shattuck Ave.,* ☎ *510/548–5049.*

$–$$ ✕ **Cafe Fanny.** Considering the low prices and high quality, people ought not complain so bitterly about the haughty, eye-rolling service and parking-lot seating of Alice Waters's chichi sandwich-and-salad joint. It's a wonderful place for lunch or dessert and coffee. ⊠ *1603 San Pablo Ave.,* ☎ *510/524–5447. No credit cards.*

$–$$ ✕ **La Méditerranée.** Arguably as queer as its same-named sister in the Castro, this bustling Middle Eastern restaurant serves huge portions of spicy, healthful food. ⊠ *2936 College Ave.,* ☎ *510/540–7773.*

$ ✕ **Berkeley Thai House.** Locals argue over which East Bay Thai restaurant deserves top billing, but almost all are good. Berkeley Thai House gets the nod here for three reasons: a tree-lined patio, its proximity to Telegraph Avenue shopping and the U.C. Berkeley campus, and low prices. ⊠ *2511 Channing Way,* ☎ *510/843–7352.*

$ ✕ **Saul's.** This old-fashioned New York–style deli in the heart of Berkeley's Gourmet Ghetto dishes up pastrami, smoked turkey breast, corned beef, knishes, potato latkes with sour cream, and other filling fare. ⊠ *1475 Shattuck Ave.,* ☎ *510/848–3354.*

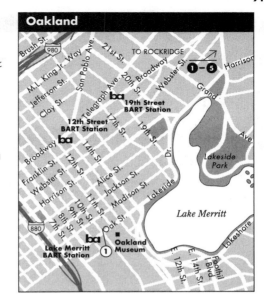

Oakland

\$\$\$ ✗ **Bay Wolf Restaurant.** Given Oakland's limited number of to-die-for dining options, it's not surprising that the Bay Wolf has packed folks in for two decades. Delicious Mediterranean–Californian cuisine includes grilled duck with ginger-peach chutney. Breakfast on the patio is a great way to start the morning. ⊠ *3853 Piedmont Ave.,* ☎ *510/655–6004.*

\$\$–\$\$\$ ✗ **Oliveto Cafe & Restaurant.** You can nosh on pizza and tapas in the boho-trendy downstairs café or settle in for traditional northern Italian cooking in the boho-snazzy upstairs dining room. Either venue has great food, good service, and a funky crowd. ⊠ *5655 College Ave.,* ☎ *510/547–5356.*

\$\$ ✗ **Nan Yang.** This restaurant serves what is arguably the Bay Area's best Burmese fare. Try the ginger salad and the garlic noodles. ⊠ *6048 College Ave.,* ☎ *510/655–3298.*

\$–\$\$ ✗ **Zachary's Chicago Pizza.** For stuffed pies you'd have to head to Chicago for greater satisfaction—the spinach-and-mushroom is a specialty. The informal pizza parlor never fails to deliver; unfortunately, you may have to wait a while for a table. ⊠ *5801 College Ave.,* ☎ *510/655–6385. No credit cards.*

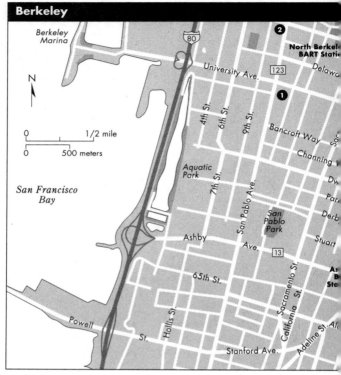

Berkeley

Berkeley Marina

Berkeley

San Francisco Bay

Aquatic Park

San Pablo Park

N

0 — 1/2 mile
0 — 500 meters

University Ave.

4th St.
6th St.
9th St.

7th St.

San Pablo Ave.

Sacramento St.

California St.

Adeline St.

Bancroft Way

Channing

Ashby Ave.

65th St.

Hollis St.

Powell St.

Stanford Ave.

North Berkele
BART Statio

Delawa

Derb

Stuart

Eats ●

Anne Kong's
World Famous
Bleach Bottle Pig
Farm, **1**
Berkeley Thai
House, **5**
Cafe Fanny, **2**

Caffe
Mediterraneum, **6**
Chez Panisse
Cafe, **4**
La
Méditerranée, **7**
Saul's, **3**

Scenes ○
White Horse, **1**

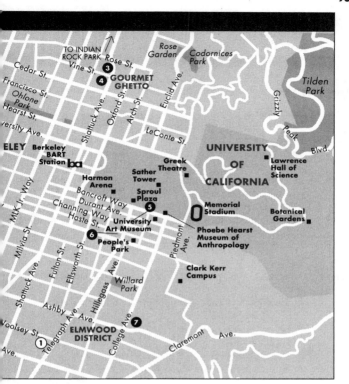

TO INDIAN
ROCK PARK Rose St.
Vine St. **3**
4 **GOURMET
GHETTO**

Cedar St.

Rose
Garden

Codornices
Park

Tilden
Park

Francisco St.
Ohlone
Park
Hearst St.

Shattuck Ave.

Oxford St.

Arch St.

Euclid Ave.

Grizzly

Peak

ersity Ave.

LeConte St.

Blvd.

ELEY Berkeley
**BART
Station** ba

UNIVERSITY

OF

CALIFORNIA

**Lawrence
Hall of
Science**

Greek
Theatre

Sather
Tower

MLK Jr. Way

**Harmon
Arena**
Bancroft Way
Durant Ave.
Channing Way
Haste St.

**Sproul
Plaza
5**

**University
Art Museum**

**Memorial
Stadium**

**Botanical
Gardens**

Milvia St.

6

**People's
Park**

Piedmont Ave.

**Phoebe Hearst
Museum of
Anthropology**

Fulton St.

Ellsworth St.

Hillegass Ave.

Willard
Park

**Clark Kerr
Campus**

Shattuck Ave.

Ashby Ave.

Woolsey St. **1** Telegraph Ave.

**ELMWOOD
DISTRICT**

College Ave.

7

Claremont Ave.

Ave.

$ ✕ **Rockridge Cafe.** Neighborhood fags and dykes brunch away at this retro diner in a hip neighborhood near Berkeley. It's a good spot for a cheap and filling lunch or early dinner (it's only open until 10). ✉ *5492 College Ave.,* ☎ *510/653–1567.*

The Peninsula

Palo Alto

$$$–   ✕ **Stars Palo Alto.** Famed San Francisco restaurateur Jeremiah
$$$$ Towers brings his cutting-edge California cuisine to a well-heeled collegiate crowd. The menu changes daily but might feature crispy-skin salmon with braised greens, or fillet of beef in a white-wine sauce with chanterelles, caramelized onions, and a potato croquette. ✉ *265 Lytton Ave.,* ☎ *415/833–1000.*

$$ ✕ **Good Earth.** It's close to a college campus and is known for its whole foods, so you'd expect the Good Earth to attract a crunchy left-wing crowd. Well, don't bet on it—this is Palo Alto. Nonetheless, the dimly lit informal dining room draws a chatty band of students and locals for eclectic fare that includes Malaysian cashew chicken, veggie couscous salads, and Greek pizza. ✉ *185 University Ave.,* ☎ *415/321–9449.*

$$ ✕ **Sushi Ya.** Sushi and sashimi fans cram into this restaurant. Soft-shell crabs and seaweed salad are among the best dishes, but everything is prepared fresh. ✉ *380 University Ave.,* ☎ *415/322–0330.*

$ ✕ **Andalé Taqueria.** The burritos at this cheap and cheerful Mexican eatery are fat, fluffy pillows of mesquite beef, barbecued pork, or vegetables. The shrimp in garlic butter with guacamole is also excellent. Don't miss the coconut flan for dessert, or the natural fruit juices prepared daily. ✉ *209 University Ave.,* ☎ *415/323–2939. No credit cards.*

Woodside

$$$ ✕ **Village Pub.** Don't confuse this trendy restaurant near Filoli for a country-village kidney-pie and ale house. It's actually a fine regional Californian restaurant with meat grills, creative starters, and a good wine selection. ✉ *2967 Woodside Rd.,* ☎ *415/851–1294.*

Half Moon Bay

$$–$$$ ✕ **Pasta Moon.** Redolent of garlic and usually packed with visiting yuppies from San Francisco, Pasta Moon is the definitive Mediterranean trattoria. Top dishes include the tagliatelle in a feather-light cream sauce with Tuscan sausage and the

chicken breast with shiitake mushrooms, prosciutto, and white wine. ⊠ *315 Main St.,* ☎ *415/726–5125.*

$$ ✕ **2 Fools Market and Cafe.** If you're passing through Half Moon Bay on an empty stomach, consider filling up on breakfast (weekends only), lunch, or dinner at this all-organic and free-range eatery. The breakfast burritos will set you up for the day. Dinner—perhaps calamari or buttermilk-roasted chicken—is healthful and light. ⊠ *408 Main St.,* ☎ *415/712–1222.*

Coffeehouse Culture

East Bay

Anne Kong's World-Famous Bleach Bottle Pig Farm. This oinker-friendly place, unusual even by Berkeley's eccentric standards, bills itself as a restaurant, coffeehouse, and pig museum. Pig photos, sculpture, and artwork abound, as do Anne Kong's own handmade pigs, fashioned out of bleach bottles. In addition to espresso and fresh baked goods, you can pick up a healthful breakfast or lunch here—the vegetarian chili, pancakes, and tofu scrambles are all good bets. It's near the fem-positive sex shop, Good Vibrations. ⊠ *2072 San Pablo Ave., Berkeley,* ☎ *510/848–7376.*

Caffe Mediterraneum. Featured prominently 30 years ago in *The Graduate,* the Med brewed both coffee and intellectual chitchat long before boutique espresso bars began turning up on every corner. The standard American fare—burgers, omelets—will do in a pinch. ⊠ *2475 Telegraph Ave., Berkeley,* ☎ *510/549–1128.*

Marin County

Depot Bookstore and Cafe. Mill Valley, home to outdoorsy aristocrats, has one of Marin County's most characterful coffeehouses. The neat and handsome Depot—a great place to pick up espressos, sandwiches, and sweets—is also a fine bookstore. ⊠ *87 Throckmorton Ave., Mill Valley,* ☎ *415/383–2665.*

The Peninsula

Printer's Inc. You can peruse any of nearly 1,000 periodicals while quaffing java at this busy coffeehouse near Stanford University. ⊠ *310 California Ave., Palo Alto,* ☎ *415/327–6500.*

SCENES

East Bay

PRIME SUSPECTS

J.R.'s. A contemporary hillside office complex in the suburb of Walnut Creek houses this typical lesbian and gay club with several small rooms, a midsize dance floor, and pool tables. Videos, a smoke machine, and strobe lights keep things lively, and the crowd is as diverse as any in the Bay Area. J.R.'s is a short walk from the Walnut Creek BART station. ✉ *2520 Camino Diablo Blvd., Walnut Creek,* ☎ *510/256–1200. Crowd: mixed m/f, mostly under 35, queerburbanites, zero-attitude, not too cruisy.*

White Horse. The thing to remember about bars in the greater Bay Area is that they're actually the most fun on weekdays, especially Thursday. Come Friday and Saturday, many regulars venture into San Francisco. Most nights at the White Horse there's a decent-size crowd, many of them students from nearby U.C. Berkeley. The place has a bar, seating, and pool tables in the front room and a dance floor in back. The staff here is plenty of fun, though because it's a college hangout, they make a big deal of checking IDs. ✉ *6551 Telegraph Ave., Oakland (near Berkeley border),* ☎ *510/652–3820. Crowd: 60/40 m/f; lots of students, a few esoteric intellectuals, alternative-music fans, neofeminists, crunchy environmentalists, gender-studies majors, etc.; also plenty of laid-back locals of all ages.*

NEIGHBORHOOD HAUNTS

Adventuras, a gay Latin dance party held on Saturdays at the **Bench & Bar** (✉ 120 11th St., Oakland, ☎ 510/444–2266), is notable for its wildly popular Latin and house tunes. The rest of the week this downtown-Oakland disco draws a young, gay, racially diverse crowd.

Marin County

Men and women—even a few straights—frequent **Aunt Ruby's** (✉ 815 W. Francisco Blvd., San Rafael, ☎ 415/459–6079), a cheerful dance and cruise bar.

The Peninsula

A nice mix of men and women shows up at **B Street** (⊠ 236 S. B St., San Mateo, ☎ 415/348–4045), a jolly bar with video screens, a patio, and dancing.

Action

Full-fledged bathhouses are still illegal in San Francisco, so the closest option (one that many S.F. residents take) is **Steamworks** (⊠ 2107 4th St., Berkeley, ☎ 510/845–8992). The crowd gets younger—mostly horny U.C. Berkeley types— as weekend evenings get toward midnight. Mondays are jumpin' here.

SLEEPS

If you're looking to take a seaside break from San Francisco, Half Moon Bay has a handful of B&Bs, two of which are extremely hospitable to gays.

For price ranges, *see* the lodging chart at the front of this guide.

Guest Houses and Small Hotels

Half Moon Bay

$$$–
$$$$ ⛩ **Cypress Inn.** Run by the talented owners of Capitola's Inn at Depot Hill (*see* Chapter 5), this contemporary property overlooks Miramar Beach and the crashing surf. The decor is coastal Californian with Southwest influences—terra-cotta tiles, skylights, and folk furniture. Both the breakfast and the afternoon hors d'oeuvres are memorable, the latter far more than a light snack. ⊠ *407 Mirada Rd., 94019, ☎ 415/726– 6002 or 800/832–3224, ℻ 415/458–2490. 8 rooms with phone and bath, most with TV. Full breakfast. Mostly straight.*

$$$–
$$$$ ⛩ **Mill Rose Inn.** This lavish, even over-the-top English coun- try–style inn has huge colorful rooms with plush furnishings, lace curtains, fresh flowers, chocolates and liqueurs, and VCRs. The innkeepers have made every attempt to make this a romantic retreat. The grounds are spectacular, with hun- dreds of flowers and blooming shrubs ⊠ *615 Mill St., 94019, ☎ 415/726–9794, ℻ 415/726–8750. 6 rooms with phone, TV, and bath. Hot tub. Full breakfast. Mostly straight.*

THE LITTLE BLACK BOOK

At Your Fingertips

Berkeley Convention and Visitors Bureau (⊠ 1834 University Ave., 94703, ☎ 510/549–7040). **Half Moon Bay Coastside Chamber of Commerce** (⊠ 520 Kelly Ave., 94019, ☎ 415/726–8380). **Marin County Convention and Visitors Bureau** (⊠ Ave. of the Flags, San Rafael, 94903, ☎ 415/472–7470). **Oakland Convention and Visitors Bureau** (⊠ 550 10th St., Suite 214, 94607, ☎ 510/839–9000). **Pacific Center** (⊠ 2712 Telegraph Ave., Berkeley, ☎ 510/841–6224; lesbian, gay, and bisexual community center serving the East Bay). **Palo Alto Chamber of Commerce** (⊠ 325 Forest Ave., 94301, ☎ 415/324–3121). **Spectrum** (⊠ 1000 Sir Francis Drake Blvd., San Anselmo, ☎ 415/457–1115; lesbian, gay, and bisexual community center serving Marin County). **West Marin Chamber of Commerce** (⊠ Box 1045, Point Reyes Station, 94956, ☎ 415/663–9232).

Gay Media

The San Francisco-based **Bay Area Reporter** and **Bay Times** (*see* The Little Black Book *in* Chapter 1) cover gay life in the areas surrounding the city. The flagship South Bay edition of **Out Now!** (☎ 408/991–1873) carries some lower-Peninsula coverage; the paper also publishes an East Bay edition.

Three mainstream alternative weeklies have some gay/lesbian coverage: Marin's **Pacific Sun** (☎ 415/383–4500), the very fine East Bay **Express** (☎ 510/540–7400), and the straight-laced **Palo Alto Weekly** (☎ 415/326–8210).

BOOKSTORES

In Oakland check out **Mama Bears** (⊠ 6536 Telegraph Ave., ☎ 510/428–9684), the Bay Area's best source of feminist and lesbian books. **Gaia Books** (⊠ 1400 Shattuck Ave., ☎ 510/548–4172) specializes in New Age, sexuality, and spirituality. **Moe's** (⊠ 2476 Telegraph Ave., ☎ 510/849–2087), a Berkeley book-buying institution, has five floors of new, antique, and just plain old tomes. Strong on lesbian, feminist, and gay titles, **Boadecia's Books** (⊠ 398 Colusa Ave., Kensington/North Berkeley, ☎ 510/559–9184) hosts stimulating readings and lectures. Marin and the Peninsula don't have any specifically gay bookstores.

3 *Out in San Jose*

L **ET'S FACE IT,** people rarely *go* to San Jose—they just end up here, on business, visiting friends, or passing through. But if you're visiting the Bay Area for the second or third time, or for more than a week, it's worth considering a day or overnight trip to sample the city's offerings. These include some decent restaurants, a healthy cultural scene, and several gay bars.

San Francisco and San Jose are connected by about 50 miles of suburban sprawl, most of it straddling I–280 and U.S. 101. The entire South Bay is highly livable, with a dry and sunny climate, good schools, a low crime rate, and a moderate cost of living. Much of America's computer boom began in the lower South Bay—Hewlett Packard, Apple, and Intel are a few of the companies that were spawned in the greater San Jose area—hence its nickname the Silicon Valley. This techy moniker conjures up images of modern offices surrounded by asphalt, but in fact San Jose has more than 125 parks, and the region as a whole is a major fruit, vegetable, and wine producer. Rugged hills form an attractive backdrop to the south, and excellent camping and hiking grounds are within a 20-minute drive of most South Bay towns.

Compared with Berkeley, San Francisco, and Santa Cruz, San Jose is conservative. Attitudes toward gays have become tolerant over the past two decades, partly because many high-tech companies have adopted enlightened policies and in part due to the influence of the South Bay's liberal neighbors. But overall, lesbian and gay visibility is extremely low.

San Jose is without an even moderately queer neighborhood, though most of its gay bars are concentrated northwest of downtown near the San Jose Arena. Some gay-popular businesses operate along The Alameda, a busy commercial drag west of downtown, and in SoFA, the revitalized arts and entertainment district south of downtown. Rainbow flags and gay pedestrians are rarely seen, however, even in these areas. Nearby Santa Clara has one of the South Bay's better bars but is otherwise devoid of queer culture.

The South Bay is big on social and professional gay groups—this is a networked and "webbed" community. A visitor just passing through will not have an easy time finding gay goings-on; even the local gay rag doesn't carry bar and restaurant listings. But many of the queers who live here couldn't be happier. Gayfolk move here in great numbers every year—not in search of a bustling nightlife or intense political community, but in search of a good job, a spacious and affordable home, and an enviable quality of life. You might say that a considerable number of people are gay in San Jose, though not all are living "gay" lives.

THE LAY OF THE LAND

The San Francisco Peninsula extends from San Francisco to San Jose. Santa Clara County, the heart of the South Bay, makes up the bulk of the peninsula's lower base and includes the cities of San Jose and Santa Clara. Santa Clara is northwest of San Jose.

San Jose

Downtown San Jose has come into its own of late. The area centered around the intersection of **Market Street** and **Santa Clara Street** was run-down and insufferably dull right through the '80s, but several years ago civic leaders and business owners teamed together to reinvent their town center. Parks were laid out and trees planted; fountains, statues, and antique-style street lamps were installed; older buildings were renovated; and new structures were built, for the most part in a sleek but carefully integrated postmodern style. For an ideal perspective on what could be called America's first true city of the 1990s, sit on the grass in **Cesar Chavez Park** (⊠ Market St., between San Fernando and San Carlos Sts.) and admire the many impressive sights around you.

San Jose is not all new. As you walk around downtown, you'll come upon several pockets of historic buildings. **Post Street,** between North 1st Street and Almaden Boulevard, for example, used to be the city's red-light district but is now picturesque, albeit with mundane shops. Definitely more lively is **San Pedro Square** and its two historic-house museums, **Peralta Adobe** (⊠ 184 W. St. John St., ☎ 408/993–8182) and **Fallon House** (⊠ 175 W. St. John St., ☎ 408/993–8182), plus a handful of restaurants and microbreweries. San Jose's one predominantly gay restaurant, Hamburger Mary's (*see* Eats *and* Scenes, *below*), is also near the square.

A bit west of San Pedro Square, beyond the highway overpass and right about where Santa Clara Street becomes **The Alameda,** is the distinctive **San Jose Arena,** the site of major sporting events and rock concerts. The arena project helped transform a former industrial wasteland into a vibrant tourist district. Aesthetically, the immense structure is problematic—its corrugated-metal exterior leaves one with the feeling of a beautiful building left unwrapped beneath.

The Alameda runs in a westerly direction from the arena before curving to the north and leading into the town of Santa Clara. Along it are a handful of restaurants and relatively funky shops, as well as the Bay Area's favorite bathhouse, the Watergarden (*see* Action, *below*), and some affordable motor lodges. Also west of downtown and below The Alameda, the **Egyptian Museum and Planetarium** (⊠ 1600 Park Ave., ☎ 408/947–3636) contains the West Coast's most impressive collection of Egyptian and Babylonian artifacts.

Back at Cesar Chavez Park, you're within walking distance of a few cultural attractions, as well as the San Jose Civic Auditorium and the San Jose Convention Center. Of the museums, one you shouldn't miss is the **San Jose Museum of Art** (⊠ 110 S. Market St., ☎ 408/294–2787), which through the year 2000 is showcasing the progress of 20th-century American art by exhibiting works from its permanent collection alongside pieces from New York's Whitney Museum. Since you're in one of the world's centers of technology, you might consider touring the **Tech Museum of Innovation** (⊠ 145 W. San Carlos St., ☎ 408/279–7150). Its hands-on exhibits survey the gadgets that will, depending on one's outlook and aptitude, either simplify or complicate our lives. The **American Museum of Quilts and Textiles** (⊠ 60 S. Market St., ☎ 408/971–0323) is not as flashy but of great interest to anyone with a bent for fashion and fabrics.

These days if a once-sucky neighborhood sprouts three coffeehouses, four art galleries, five nightclubs, and six trendy restaurants, it's given a catchy, usually four-letter nickname. San Francisco has SoMa, Manhattan has SoHo, Denver has LoDo, and San Jose has SoFA—which stands for "South of First (Street) Area." SoFA has a gay feel to it, in the same way San Francisco's SoMa does, but it's not all that queer. There are shops and restaurants along South 1st Street from Santa Clara Street down to Reed Street, but SoFA's nightlife is concentrated in the lower half of this stretch, below San Carlos Street.

To gain a sense of life in the South Bay before the computer chip, head a couple of miles southeast of downtown to 25-acre **Kelley Park,** site of the **San Jose Historical Museum** (⊠ 1600 Senter Rd., ☎ 408/287–2290). About two-dozen mostly Victorian buildings—half of them original and half rebuilt, can be toured here, including a trolley barn, a doctor's office, and a post office. Also in Kelley Park is the **Japanese Friendship Garden.**

Of San Jose's many ethnic enclaves, **Japantown,** which is north of downtown, is the one most visited by tourists. Along the 200 block of Jackson Street are many restaurants, plus numerous shops and a handful of historic buildings.

Santa Clara

Edward Scissorhands could easily have been filmed in any of the plain though not unpleasant residential neighborhoods of **Santa Clara.** The **Mission Santa Clara de Assis,** the eighth of California's 21 late-18th-century missions, was built in 1777. It now anchors the campus of Jesuit **Santa Clara University** (⊠ 500 El Camino Real, ☎ 408/554–4023), which was founded in 1851 as California's first university. You can wander amid the mission's remaining buildings (the original chapel burned but a replica stands in its place). The university's **de Saisset Museum** (☎ 408/554–4528) contains many mission artifacts, old master and contemporary art, and the definitive collection of works by the early 20th-century painter Henrietta Shore.

The **Intel Museum** (⊠ Robert Noyce Bldg., 2200 Mission College Blvd., ☎ 408/765–0503) reveals just how much the world has changed since Santa Clara's mission days. Billing itself as a showcase of "Technology for the Technophobic," the museum nevertheless focuses on some weighty concepts, from the development of microprocessing to how semiconductors work.

Paramount's Great America (⊠ Great America Pkwy., off U.S. 101, ☎ 408/988–1776) theme park has state-of-the-art rides and amusements. An unofficial "gay day" has been held here in the past, usually in the fall; check *Out Now!* (*see* Gay Media *in* The Little Black Book, *below*).

Santa Clara is basically a yawn when it comes to strolling, though the town center has many historic homes and buildings. Park near the intersection of Main and Fremont streets and explore the surrounding blocks.

GETTING AROUND

The driving time from San Francisco to Santa Clara is about 50 minutes; it takes a little more than an hour to get to downtown San Jose. Both I–280 and U.S. 101 will get you there, but the latter has more traffic and is less scenic. **Cal-Train** (☎ 800/660–4287), a commuter service, stops in San Jose and Santa Clara. San Jose's outstanding **Light Rail System** (☎ 408/321–2300) runs from Santa Clara in the north through downtown San Jose before ending in the southeast. Driving is the easiest way to get around the area, though parking and traffic in the center of San Jose can be difficult; if exploring this area is your goal, consider parking north of downtown near 1st Street and taking light rail the rest of the way. Stations are located along 1st Street.

WHEN TO GO

In May San Jose hosts one of the largest **Cinco de Mayo** (☎ 408/977–0900) celebrations in the country. **Gay pride** (☎ 408/293–2429) is always the first or second week in June. Every July the little town of Gilroy, about 30 miles south of San Jose, hosts the **Gilroy Garlic Festival** (☎ 408/842–6436)—if you're a fan of these aromatic little bulbs, you won't be disappointed. Gilroy is nicknamed the Garlic Capital of the World.

EATS

Compared to San Francisco, the Wine Country, or Berkeley, the South Bay has a tame dining scene. Not that there aren't decent places to eat, but food isn't a reason in itself to visit. And other than Hamburger Mary's in San Jose, few places have visibly gay followings. Owing to San Jose's strong ethnic influences, especially Asian and Mexican, you will find excellent international options.

For price ranges, *see* the dining chart at the front of this guide.

San Jose

$$$$ ✕ **Emile's.** Swiss expat Emile Mooser presides over what many consider the top restaurant in San Jose, delivering a mix of traditional and nouvelle contemporary cuisine in a dining room filled with fresh flowers and formal furnishings. House-cured gravlax and roast loin of venison are a few dishes that harken back to Europe, but Emile's also serves such otherworldly fare as seared ahi with rice vinegar and soy sauce. ✉ *545 S. 2nd St.,* ☎ *408/289–1960.*

$$–$$$ ✕ **Eulipia.** Eclectic in both its menu and its clientele, this staple of San Jose's SoFA renaissance draws the post-theater crowd, corporate types, and a few high-end club kids. Asian, Mexican, Continental, and regional flavors appear on the menu in dazzling creations, among them mesquite-grilled polenta and fresh vegetables. ✉ *374 S. 1st St.,* ☎ *408/280–6161.*

$$ ✕ **Hamburger Mary's.** Of the several Mary's on the West Coast, this one may play the most significant role within its queer community. Though it's patronized by straights as well, this is *the* gay restaurant, and also the main place for socializing and late-night dancing. In addition to several lounges and a disco, there are two large dining rooms, one of them littered with every conceivable form of bric-a-brac from clown paintings to Tonka Toy dump trucks to '50s magazine advertisements. A sprawling patio with tropical plants is the focal point of an indoor–outdoor eating area. The menu is typical of the chain, with killer burgers (veggie versions can be substituted) and other basic pub grub. ✉ *170 W. St. John St.,* ☎ *408/947–1667.*

$$ ✕ **71 St. Peter.** An outstanding wine list, reasonable prices, and a warm country-house atmosphere contribute to this

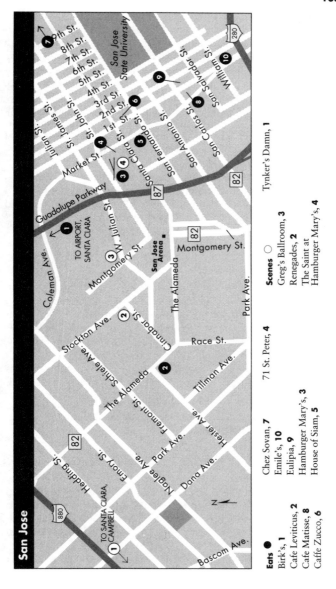

San Jose

Eats ●
Birk's, **1**
Cafe Leviticus, **2**
Cafe Matisse, **8**
Caffe Zucco, **6**

Chez Sovan, **7**
Emile's, **10**
Eulipia, **9**
Hamburger Mary's, **3**
House of Siam, **5**

71 St. Peter, **4**

Scenes ○
Greg's Ballroom, **3**
Renegades, **2**
The Saint at
Hamburger Mary's, **4**

Tynker's Damn, **1**

restaurant's success. The food happens to be delicious, too. The menu is divided into four categories: first courses, salads, pastas, and main courses. Grilled and roasted duck with a potato-leek cake and raspberry–black pepper demi-glace is one of the best entrées; of pastas the simple porcini ravioli with sage brown butter scores high. Terrific desserts, too. ⊠ *71 N. San Pedro St.,* ☎ *408/971–8523.*

$–$$ ✕ **House of Siam.** The chefs at this downtown restaurant aren't afraid to go heavy on the hot spices but will also grant your request for milder seasoning. Standout dishes include the beef salad, several vegetarian curries, and pad thai. ⊠ *55 S. Market St.,* ☎ *408/279–5668.*

$ ✕ **Chez Sovan.** In a city blessed with ethnic diversity this is one of the culinary stars. The Cambodian menu is long and detailed, with traditional stews, cilantro- and mint-infused salads, and spicy catfish, pork, and chicken dishes. ⊠ *923 Old Oakland Rd.,* ☎ *408/287–7619.*

Santa Clara

$$$ ✕ **Birk's.** By no means a major Bay Area culinary outpost, Santa Clara does lay claim to this suave supper spot created by San Francisco restaurant guru Pat Kuleto. A bar in front serves single-malt Scotches and microbrews. The food is New American with various regional nods. Fresh fish grills and rotisserie-smoked chicken are a few dependables. Birk's is set inside a modern office building, but its handsome interior is surprisingly warm. ⊠ *3955 Freedom Cir., at U.S. 101 and Great America Pkwy.,* ☎ *408/980–6400.*

Coffeehouse Culture

San Jose

Cafe Leviticus. Without question this beanery inside a stately old converted bank is the queerest in the South Bay. Plenty of alternative-looking breeders stop by, too. You can pick up the gay paper here, and occasional fliers on upcoming events. Unfortunately the tables in this imposing space are far apart, making it lousy for mingling. ⊠ *1445 The Alameda,* ☎ *408/279–8877.*

Cafe Matisse. This sophisticated sidewalk SoFA boîte draws a regular flow of club goers and artsy types for late-night desserts or coffees. But don't overlook Matisse for lunch—

fresh salads, homemade soups, and inventive sandwiches. ⊠ *371 S. 1st St.,* ☎ *408/298–7788.*

Caffe Zucco. Though it's nowhere near as queer as Cafe Leviticus, this is a hopping juice and espresso joint on increasingly trendy South 1st. Smoothies come in such refreshing combinations as the mango tango—pineapple, passion fruit, and mango—and the Maya papaya, which blends coconuts, bananas, and papayas. Pastries, salads, and panini sandwiches are also served. ⊠ *74 S. 1st St.,* ☎ *408/ 297–9777.*

SCENES

San Jose nightlife finally developed over the past decade to the point where its residents no longer have to drive an hour to San Francisco to find things to do. Hard-partying locals still head north on weekends, but San Jose bars stay fairly crowded, too. Nonetheless, for a city of 850,000, gay nightlife options are limited. There aren't any warehouse-style discos, but a few spots have decent-size dance floors. There's no longer a full-time dyke bar—Selections, in an industrial neighborhood north of town, has gone straight—but as elsewhere women patronize some predominantly male bars. The only South Bay gay bar outside San Jose is in nearby Santa Clara, and it's one of the region's more popular. In general, the bar culture is low-key and down-to-earth. Stand-and-model types will have a better time in San Francisco.

Near the Arena

PRIME SUSPECTS

Greg's Ballroom. This rickety old bar and disco, the town's favorite after Hamburger Mary's, is inside a modest house directly behind the San Jose Arena. You enter into a horseshoe-shape bar with seats around it; beyond this is the small dance floor. The decor consists of four walls—Greg's is not a flashy place. Its best attribute is the large deck out back. ⊠ *511 W. Julian St.,* ☎ *408/286–4388. Crowd: 85/15 m/f; all ages, racially diverse; friendly; mix of regular joes, blue collars, and computer specialists.*

Renegades. A dark shanty with zero ambience and a mix of pierced club kids and hairy leather daddies, Renegades bears an amazing resemblance to San Francisco's Hole in the Wall

Saloon. There's a long bar on one side, a pool table to the right, and games in back. Throughout are chairs and tables, many of which appear on the verge of falling apart. Out the back door is a patio. If you think the South Bay lacks an edge, you need to come here. This is the sort of place where a guy will make a pass at you by putting out his cigarette on the back of your hand. ⊠ *393 Stockton Ave.,* ☎ *408/275–9902. Crowd: male; mostly 30s and 40s; diverse, mixed racially; leather, flannel and ripped jeans; bears; tattoos, piercings.*

The Saint at Hamburger Mary's. The Saint is actually a long, rectangular disco inside the Hamburger Mary's restaurant. It's the most popular dance club in town, but usually not until after 11 PM. Hamburger Mary's itself has a few cozy lounges. One has video screens, booths, and a long bar; the room beyond that has pinball machines, video games, and a pool table. Both are excellent places to hang out with old friends or meet new ones. Overall, this is the most lesbian-favored club in San Jose, though it's still largely male. ⊠ *170 W. St. John St.,* ☎ *408/947–1667. Crowd at the Saint: 70/30 m/f, fairly young but with plenty of exceptions, energetic, loud. Crowd in lounges: 60/40 m/f, more diverse than at the Saint, quieter, very approachable.*

NEIGHBORHOOD HAUNTS

641 (⊠ 641 Stockton Ave., ☎ 408/998–1144) is especially popular with Hispanic and African-American men and to a lesser degree lesbians. From the outside it looks like a little shack, but the bar actually extends pretty far back, where there's a dance floor and a great patio beyond that. The club's beer bust the first and third Sunday of every month draws a good crowd; it's promoted rather strangely as "The Bitch's House." **Buck's** (⊠ 301 Stockton Ave., ☎ 408/286–1176) is a darker and even seedier version of Renegades.

SoFA

The emergence of **SoFA** has given San Jose a few more nightlife options, but with the exception of the small but popular gay dive **Mac's** (⊠ 349 S. 1st St., ☎ 408/998–9535), none of these establishments is even half queer. The **Usual** (⊠ 400 S. 1st St., ☎ 408/298–9375) changes its identity constantly; it typically draws an alternative and somewhat gay-friendly crowd, and occasionally hosts queer dance parties. Across the street the

Agenda (✉ 399 S. 1st St., ☎ 408/287–4087), an old-fashioned jazz lounge, is accepting of all types.

Santa Clara

PRIME SUSPECT

Tynker's Damn. Known by locals as T.D.'s, this upbeat and crowded video bar has a small dance floor, plenty of seating at tables and at the bar, and a friendly staff. It draws a younger bunch than the San Jose bars, many of them guys from the several nearby universities. After T.D.'s closes, lots of fellas congregate in the parking lot, slowly cruising around—in both senses of the word—for as long as two hours. Perhaps no bar on the West Coast has a more formalized ritual of car cruising. ✉ *46 N. Saratoga Ave., at Stevens Creek Blvd.,* ☎ *408/243–4595. Crowd: mostly male, mostly under 35, collegiate, a few poseurs, some guppies.*

Action

San Jose's men's club and bathhouse, the **Watergarden** (✉ 1010 The Alameda, ☎ 408/275–1215) is so spiffy and well run that many customers come all the way from San Francisco. The extensive facility has a large deck and pool, private and group rooms, showers and steam rooms, and saunas and workout facilities. On weekends after the bars close, business really picks up, but the place is often packed on sunny afternoons as well. San Jose has a first-rate queer sex shop, **Leather Masters** (✉ 969 Park Ave., ☎ 408/293–7660).

SLEEPS

With few exceptions most South Bay hotels cater to business travelers. There are few B&Bs and no gay-specific accommodations.

For price ranges, *see* the lodging chart at the front of this guide.

San Jose

$$$$ 🏨 **The Fairmont.** It may not be as historic or as full of character as its famous namesake on San Francisco's Nob Hill, but the San Jose branch is a very fine property. Relatively new, it has a first-rate business center, a 58-foot pool with an ample patio, and spacious rooms with goose-down pillows, walk-in closets, and other thoughtful touches. It doesn't get any better in these parts. ⊠ *170 S. Market St., 95113,* ☎ *408/998–1900 or 800/527–4727,* FAX *408/287–1648. 500 rooms, 41 suites. 4 restaurants, pool.*

$$$ 🏨 **Hotel De Anza.** This 1931 art deco skyscraper is one of the most distinctive buildings downtown. The perfectly pleasant rooms unfortunately lack the character expected in a historic hotel, though they are outfitted with such modern perks as VCRs and TVs in the bathrooms. ⊠ *233 W. Santa Clara St., 95113,* ☎ *408/286–1000 or 800/843–3700,* FAX *408/286–0500. 100 rooms. Restaurant.*

$$–$$$ 🏨 **The Arena Hotel.** The Arena is first-rate in every regard. Its attractively furnished rooms have VCRs and CD stereo systems, plus refrigerators, microwaves, and coffeemakers. ⊠ *817 The Alameda, 95126,* ☎ *408/294–6500 or 800/882–1984,* FAX *408/294–6585. 89 rooms. Restaurant.*

$ 🏨 **San Jose Sports Arena Travelodge.** Should you not wish to spend the night in the Watergarden bathhouse, you can always stay a couple of doors down at this simple chain motel. ⊠ *1041 The Alameda, 95126,* ☎ *408/295–0159 or 800/255–3050,* FAX *408/998–5509. 65 rooms. Pool.*

THE LITTLE BLACK BOOK

At Your Fingertips

Billy DeFrank Lesbian and Gay Community Center (⊠ 175 Stockton Ave., San Jose, ☎ 408/293–2429 for events listings). **Santa Clara Chamber of Commerce and Convention & Visitors Bureau** (⊠ 2200 Laurelwood Rd., 95054, ☎ 408/970–9825). **Santa Clara Visitors Center** (⊠ 1515 El Camino Real, ☎ 408/296–7111). **San Jose Convention and Visitors Bureau** (⊠ 333 W. San Carlos St., Suite 1000, ☎ 408/295–9600 or 800/726–5673).

Gay Media

Silicon Valley queers look to the biweekly ***Out Now!*** (☎ 408/991–1873) for outstanding coverage of local and national gay news. Virtually no space is dedicated to entertainment (so don't pick it up expecting bar tips).

The best and most comprehensive arts and entertainment weekly in the Santa Clara valley is ***Metro*** (☎ 408/298–8000); it has occasional gay and lesbian events listings.

No gay bookstores operate in the South Bay, though most of the chain bookstores have gay and lesbian sections. But if you're looking for an extensive selection of queer reading material, stick to San Francisco or nearby Santa Cruz.

Working Out

There being no gay gym in downtown San Jose, your best bet is in the town of Campbell at the **World Gym** (⊠ 2290 S. Winchester Blvd., ☎ 408/278–0343).

4 *Out in* the Russian River and the Wine Country

THE RUSSIAN RIVER VALLEY, northern California's premier gay resort, is sleepy, slightly ragged, and blessed with a canopy of redwoods. During this century it's been home to loggers, bikers, hippies, and Mexican immigrants, and before that to Russian fur trappers and the Pomo Indians. After a couple of gay men opened bed-and-breakfasts in the '70s, the town of Guerneville boomed with activity, and queerfolk replaced families as the River's most visible summertime visitors. Even in wilder times the atmosphere was folksier and less club-oriented than in Key West or P-town, but many gays liked the area so much they ended up buying property.

That the Russian River's lesbian and gay settlers will always love it here is a foregone conclusion. Less certain is the region's status as a queer destination. Unfortunately, what inevitably gets billed as the "flood of the century" ravages the area every decade or so. There was a terrible deluge in 1984, two equally devastating ones during the winter of 1994–95, and heavy flooding in the winter of 1997.

A few restaurants, resorts, and other businesses fold after the floods, but most rebuild better than ever—Russian Riverites are a resilient bunch. Tourists on the other hand are more fickle. Though many loyal regulars continue to return, the overall number of visitors has dropped. The permanent community seems as strong as ever—the gay and lesbian stamp on the area is evident everywhere—but success in attracting younger queers has been spotty at best.

People at the River don't spend huge amounts on fine dining or fancy retreats. This is where you head when big-city living starts to get to you. There's nothing more peaceful than floating down the river on a raft or an inner tube on a sunny day. You can also canoe the river ("the upper-body workout with a view," says one local) or hike among the redwood groves in Armstrong Woods and other parks. If you're the more sedentary type, you'll find enough sundecks and swimming pools to model that figure you've been perfecting, and plenty of fun-loving queens to party with. And don't let stories of torrential rains and flooding put you off—storms come only in winter; the rest of the year can be right beautiful.

Many gay people combine a trip to the River with one to California's premier winegrowing region. The Wine Country of the Napa and Sonoma valleys is not a gay stopover per se— the nearest bar is in Santa Rosa, for instance, and there aren't the same types of resorts one finds along the Russian River. But you'll find queerfolk everywhere: tasting wine, dining in some of northern California's most highly touted restaurants, and indulging in rejuvenating spa treatments.

The Wine Country is generally a sophisticated place, the Napa Valley in particular, so you're not likely to feel uncomfortable. With all the media coverage of lesbians and gays in the Bay Area, everyone has seen a homo or two—you won't be the novelty you might be elsewhere. And at the mud bath and other spas, your orientation leaves you at a distinct advantage: Most segregate patrons by gender. (There's nothing more romantic than wallowing in a heap of peat or volcanic ash with honey beside you in the next tub.)

Romantic options abound—you can splurge on a hot-air balloon ride, enjoy a walk through leafy Jack London State Park, or window-shop in Healdsburg or St. Helena. Unlike San Francisco, evenings in late spring, all summer, and in early fall are often warm, making dining alfresco a definite possibility. The Napa Valley tends to be more congested than its Sonoma counterpart; you need to strategize so as not to waste time (tips are provided below), but except on busy weekends both areas are easily maneuvered.

THE LAY OF THE LAND

Sonoma County encompasses a large block of northern California; it's directly north of Marin County and west of Napa County. Most people think of the winegrowing region that abuts Napa's when they think of Sonoma, but the county also includes coastal towns such as Bodega Bay and Jenner, the Russian River communities of Guerneville and Monte Rio, and the smallish cities of Santa Rosa and Petaluma.

The points covered in this chapter appear relatively close on a map, but be aware that roads, though not treacherous, are often narrow and winding. In theory you can drive from Bodega Bay to Calistoga in 90 minutes, but this is prime territory for back road exploring—plan to tour no more than a few communities, or three or four wineries, in a day to leave yourself time to appreciate the varied scenery.

Western Sonoma County is like Germany's Black Forest: opaque, dense, mysterious, and heavy. Eastern Sonoma County, where more of the grapes are grown, is like Aix-en-Provence or Tuscany: clear, expansive, manifest, and light. In both halves, there is immense beauty. The coastal span is a virtual rain forest, alive with exotic flowers and blooming shrubs shaded by towering redwoods and aromatic pines. As you head east into the heart of the Wine Country, beyond the city of Santa Rosa, the hills soften, and a moderately dry climate prevails. Vast expanses of blue sky dominate the horizon, and tall trees become more sparse as you continue onward to the even drier Napa Valley. The valley's foothills are a rich green during normal winters, but come summer they're golden, the main color coming from the light-green grape leaves in the vineyards.

Guerneville and Monte Rio

Quirky **Guerneville** and **Monte Rio,** home to the Russian River's main gay and lesbian resorts, seem almost frozen in time. Guerneville, with 7,000 people, is much larger than Monte Rio. Except for a handful of wineries and some crafts galleries, there aren't many cultural attractions: People come to canoe, hike, or lie in the sun at beaches along the river or on sundecks at the resorts. Aging hippies and left-leaning thinkers make up a significant chunk of both the visiting and permanent population; about every sixth car is an old VW bus.

Russian River is not a place to sashay about in your finest threads or to brag about who you know or where your career is headed. Bars are attitude-free, even a little rowdy, and snootiness is not tolerated. You're here to chill out. As the menu at Guerneville's grub joint the Hiding Place says, "If you're not served in 10 minutes . . . relax! You'll be served in 15 or maybe 30 minutes."

Guerneville is where you'll find the only nightlife and most of the restaurants and accommodations. It's not a shopping mecca, but there are some offbeat stores downtown. **Up the River** (⊠ 16212 Main St., ☎ 707/869–3167) carries both tasteful and unabashedly tasteless cards and gifts. **Memories That Linger** (⊠ 16218 Main St., ☎ 707/869–2971) sells lingerie, clothing, and other fun stuff. The town holds a few antiques stores, including **Wayne Scala's Antiques** (⊠ 14081 Mill St., ☎ 707/869–0513), **R.F. Antiques and Eccentricities** (⊠ 13550 Church St., ☎ 707/869–1021), and **The Royal Barge** (⊠ 16270 Main St., ☎ 707/869–1228).

The 800-acre **Armstrong Redwoods State Reserve** (⊠ 17000 Armstrong Woods Rd., ☎ 707/869–2015 or 707/865–2391) is home to some of the tallest and oldest trees in northern California, including the 310-foot Parson Jones tree and the 1,400-year-old Colonel James Armstrong Tree. You'll also discover an abundance of tan oaks, California laurels, and big-leaf maples. The logging industry having stripped away much of the state's ancient forest, this park is testimony to what once was. Stop by the visitor center for excellent trail maps and advice, or sit in the Redwood Forest amphitheater, a tranquil spot to let the awesome beauty of the forest consume you. Also consider seeing the park on horseback; contact the **Armstrong Woods Pack Station** (☎ 707/887–2939). Half-day and full-day rides are given, as well as one- to three-night trips.

You won't go wrong on any expedition arranged through **Burke's Canoe Trips** (⊠ 8600 River Rd., Forestville, ☎ 707/887–1222). You paddle west with the current, and the company retrieves you and the canoe just east of Guerneville.

You might also want to cast a line into this river known for its salmon, shad, bass, and catfish. The staff at **King's Sport and Tackle** (⊠ 16258 Main St., ☎ 707/869–2156) will tell you where they're biting.

If you don't care to drive a long way to taste the grape, there are a few smaller wineries nearby, including **Mark West Estate** (⊠ 7010 Trenton–Healdsburg Rd., Forestville, ☎ 707/544–4813). For a change of pace from River lounging, take the tour at the **Korbel Champagne Cellars** (⊠ 13250 River Rd., Guerneville, ☎ 707/887–2294), which is headquartered in a century-old, creeper-covered brick building. You'll get a solid overview of the history and process of champagne making.

Just southeast of Guerneville, on Highway 116, is little **Forestville,** which has a couple of unique attractions. One is the outstanding French bistro **Chez Marie** (*see* Eats, *below*). The other is **California Carnivores of Forestville** (⊠ 7020 Trenton–Healdsburg Rd., ☎ 707/838–1630). Not a steak house (or a sex club), this is allegedly—fans of *Little Shop of Horrors* take note—the nation's largest nursery of carnivorous plants, where you can buy a meat eater to take back home. Tours are available.

Coastal Sonoma County

From Guerneville, Highway 116 snakes alongside the Russian River for about 15 miles before emptying into the Pacific just below the village of **Jenner,** home to a handful of inns and restaurants. The 13 miles south from here to Bodega Bay are lined with windswept shoreline, starting with **Goat Rock State Beach,** where a colony of seals holds court part of the year. This coastal stretch is ideal for beachcombing and hiking, but a bit rough for swimming and typically too cool and windy to attract many sunbathers.

Bodega Bay, where Suzanne Pleshette received an unceremonious pecking in Alfred Hitchcock's *The Birds,* remains a laid-back commercial fishing village of clapboard houses and unprepossessing shops. Not surprisingly, it's an excellent place for bird-watching. Depending on the time of year, you'll be inundated—but probably not fatally attacked—by plovers, killdeer, willets, curlews, and seagulls. Catch a quick bite at the restaurant at the **Inn at the Tides** (⊠ 800 Hwy. 1, ☎ 707/875–2751), where fresh seafood comes in both trendy and old-fashioned configurations. If you're in a hurry or just want to nosh, grab some smoked fish or salmon jerky to go at **The Crab Pot** (⊠ 1750 Hwy. 1, ☎ 707/875–9970), a mile to the north.

Head north of Jenner for 11 miles along an equally impressive section of Highway 1 to reach **Fort Ross State Historic Park** (☎ 707/847–3286), a re-created trading outpost settled in 1812 by Russian fur trappers (Ross is an armchair name for Russia). The fort was established as an outpost of the Russians' considerably more substantial settlement at Sitka (in what is now Alaska). For 30 years they explored the Sonoma region, bartering with Yankees, Mexicans, and indigenous Pomo Indians and hunting down the native sea otter, nearly to the point of extinction. In 1841 they sold their extensive land holdings to John Sutter, who later became famous when gold was discovered in 1848 on his property in eastern California. The grounds consist of second-growth redwoods and numerous stands of Bishop pine and Douglas firs; exhibits trace the fort's history and that of the Pomo natives.

A few miles north is **Salt Point State Park** (⊠ Hwy. 1, ☎ 707/847–3221), which holds the remnants of many Pomo villages, plus extensive hiking trails and a pygmy forest. Just to Salt Point's north is the 317-acre **Kruse Rhododendron State Reserve** (⊠ Hwy. 1, ☎ 707/847–3221). Some of its many native rhododendrons grow as tall as 30 feet. Douglas fir and redwoods loom hauntingly over the pink flowering bushes, which bloom in April and May.

To return to Guerneville, consider this tortuous but gorgeous route: From the Kruse Reserve, head inland on Kruse Ranch Road, turn right onto Seaview Road and then left onto Fort Ross Road. Eventually you'll pass through the wooded hamlet of **Cazadero.** Here turn right onto the Cazadero Highway, which winds down several miles back to Highway 116, close to Monte Rio.

Southern Sonoma County

South of Monte Rio and Guerneville are a couple of towns worth exploring, Sebastopol and Occidental. **Sebastopol,** at the junction of highways 12 and 116, has some pick-your-own farms. On weekends, carloads of queens head down here to browse through **Midgley's Country Flea Market** (⊠ 2200 Gravenstein Hwy. S, ☎ 707/823–7874). For more serious pieces, and still plenty of affordable bric-a-brac, try the **Sebastopol Antique Mall** (⊠ 755 Petaluma Ave., ☎ 707/823–1936).

Heading south from Monte Rio the Bohemian Highway meanders past the notorious Bohemian Grove—where America's movers and shakers unwind (and occasionally perform in drag shows)—toward tiny **Occidental,** an old redwood-logging village with antiques dealers, crafts and art galleries, turn-of-the-century homes, and **Howard's Cafe Bakery and Juice Bar** (⊠ 75 Main St., ☎ 707/874–2838), a mellow hangout with indoor and outdoor seating. The town also sponsors a fine chamber music and arts program.

Historic **Petaluma,** inland along Sonoma County's southern border off U.S. 101, is loaded with Victorian and turn-of-the-century homes—it has one of the highest such concentrations in the region. A restored 300-passenger paddle wheeler is docked downtown on the Petaluma River, testimony to this small city's early history as a major river port. Walking through the Americana-infused streets of Winona Ryder's hometown you'll think you could be just about anywhere in the country—sure enough, the neighborhood scenes in *American Graffiti* and *Peggy Sue Got Married* were filmed here.

Santa Rosa

Santa Rosa, population 115,000, is not devoid of charm, but there's little reason to spend more than a day here. Directly between the Napa and Sonoma valleys and the Russian River and western Sonoma towns, it's a good place to find shops, services, and inexpensive chain hotels.

Historic **Railroad Square,** just west of U.S. 101 and north of Highway 12 between 3rd and 5th streets, is a perhaps-too-quaint complex of stone and brick late-19th-century buildings that house shops and cafés. More worth your time is the vibrant **Luther Burbank Home and Gardens** (⊠ Santa Rosa and Sonoma Aves., ☎ 707/524–5445), the fascinating compound of the renowned horticulturist. The **Luther Burbank Center for the Arts** (⊠ 50 Mark West Springs Rd., ☎ 707/ 546–3600) is the area's major venue for cultural events.

The Sonoma Valley

Wine making was early a Sonoma tradition, begun first by the visiting Russians of Fort Ross and the early Catholics who set up a mission here in the early 1820s. The tradition was advanced to new levels by Mexican General Mariano Vallejo, who presided over the then Mexican land that comprises the

Sonoma Valley, and later by a Hungarian immigrant, Count Agoston Haraszthy. The count, who's acknowledged today as the father of the state's wine industry, was one of the first in the area to visit Europe in search of new varieties of grapes and bring them back to California.

Sonoma's main winegrowing region runs parallel to and west of Napa's for about 30 miles, from the town of Sonoma north to Healdsburg. Vineyards remain abundant for 15 miles or so north of Healdsburg, through the communities of Geyserville and Cloverdale. In the southern half of the region, follow scenic Highway 12 as far as Santa Rosa. To reach the northern towns, take U.S. 101.

Among northern California towns, **Sonoma** is something of an anomaly, feeling equal parts southern California, New Mexico, and northern Italy. Spanish Mission–style architecture dominates downtown, which is anchored by Sonoma Plaza, an animated town green that would look right at home in Santa Fe. You may recognize Sonoma City Hall—it doubled as the Tuscany County Courthouse in TV's *Falcon Crest.*

You can eat at any of two-dozen places on the plaza, or drop by the **Sonoma Cheese Factory** (✉ 2 Spain St., ☎ 707/996–1931) to pick up a little of wine's favorite companion, locally made jack cheese (free samples abound). There's also a deli inside. For some of the freshest food around, stop by the **Sonoma Farmers' Market,** held Friday 9 to noon in Depot Park and again on Tuesday night in the Sonoma Plaza from 4:30 until sunset. Not far from Sonoma Plaza lies **Mission San Francisco Solano de Sonoma,** the northernmost of California's 21 Catholic missions and one of several early-19th-century structures within **Sonoma State Historic Park** (✉ 114 Spain St. E, ☎ 707/938–1519).

Most Sonoma Wine Country visitors tour the 17-mile-long Valley of the Moon, from Sonoma up through the towns of **Glen Ellen** and **Kenwood.** Novelist, itinerant worker, and socialist Jack London hailed from here and gave the region its lunar nickname (it's also the name of one of his novels). You can visit his grave and the cottage in which he penned many of his works at **Jack London State Historical Park** (✉ 2400 London Ranch Rd., Glen Ellen, ☎ 707/938–5216). Writer M.F.K. Fisher also lived in Glen Ellen for a time.

The charming town of **Healdsburg** looks and feels the way many now-overdeveloped ones in Napa once did. Healdsburg is growing rapidly, too, and has a burgeoning wine industry. As in Sonoma, activity centers around a vibrant Spanish-influenced green, which is shaded by an odd mix of palm and redwood trees. Unlike other towns in the Wine Country, Healdsburg has a discernible, if not concentrated, gay and lesbian population.

Downtown Healdsburg's dapper streets invite strolling. Because the town has yet to become overrun by tourists, its shopkeepers and restaurateurs are likely to spend a little more time chatting with you than elsewhere in the region. The **Healdsburg Museum** (✉ 221 Matheson St., ☎ 707/431–3325), housed inside an imposing 1910 former library, exhibits local artifacts, including 8,000 original photographs.

The Napa Valley

Broad and flat, the Napa Valley has scenery that is pleasant if not quite as lush as Sonoma's. You come here mainly to visit the star wineries and restaurants. The valley runs about 30 miles, from the town of Napa in the south to Calistoga in the north. Two primary roads traverse the valley. Commercial wineries line traffic-clogged Highway 29 like rows of car dealers. Running parallel 1 to 3 miles east, the delightful and less-crowded Silverado Trail skirts the valley's eastern foothills. Many fine though for the most part lesser-known wineries are along this road.

The Wappo Indians were the Napa Valley's original settlers. Father José Altimira investigated the valley in 1823 as a potential site for the northernmost of California's missions (the nearby town of Sonoma later earned this distinction). Shortly after Altimira passed through, settler George Yount planted a small vineyard to produce wine for his family.

In 1858 Charles Krug, a German immigrant who had witnessed the success of Count Haraszthy in the Sonoma Valley, surmised that the Napa Valley would also support wine making. Other vintners followed suit when his hunch turned out right. By the latter part of the 19th century, German grapes had been introduced to the region, which was also being mined for silver and cinnabar (quicksilver).

The Napa Valley wine industry boomed throughout the early part of the 20th century, took a dive during Prohibition, boomed again following its repeal, and had pretty much revived by the early '60s. After a Stag's Leap cabernet sauvignon won a blind taste test in France in 1976, the Napa Valley began to attain world-class status; Sonoma's rise to prominence followed shortly thereafter. Over the past two decades a few hundred wineries have opened in the two valleys, though interestingly more than 90% of the state's wine (i.e., the sort of liquid dross that comes in a jug) is produced not here but in central California.

Downtown **Napa,** a grim experiment in '60s and '70s bunker-style architecture, should be skipped. Most of the wineries and restaurants are north of downtown, along Highway 29. Also along this stretch, **Red Hen Antiques** (⊠ 5091 St. Helena Hwy., ☎ 707/257–0822) houses more than 70 stalls. The excellent **Napa Valley Farmers' Market** is held in Napa at 1st and Pearl streets on Tuesdays 7:30 to noon. There's also one in St. Helena at the Old Railroad Depot (⊠ Adams St.) on Friday mornings from 7:30 to 11:30.

Upon reaching **Yountville** you can browse the 40 shops at **Vintage 1870** (⊠ 6525 Washington St., ☎ 707/944–2451), a massive brick château that was once the home of early wine maker Gottlieb Groezinger and is now a yuppie-infested shopping village. The town of Yountville is anchored by historic Washington Square, just off Highway 29, which is also home to shops and boutiques.

The two towns north of here, **Oakville** and **Rutherford,** hold several top wineries. One of the least-traveled but most rewarding drives connects the Napa and Sonoma valleys. The half-hour trek begins on the **Oakville Grade,** just south of Rutherford at its junction with Highway 29. Follow the road up a steep, twisting hill until it joins with Dry Creek Road and eventually Trinity Road, which winds just as precipitously down to Highway 12 in Glen Ellen.

In **St. Helena** you can investigate Wine Country history at the **Napa Valley Museum** (⊠ 473 Main St., ☎ 707/963–7411). Permanent exhibitions include photos, artifacts, and documents tracing back 4,000 years to the arrival of the Wappo Indians. Nearby is the **Silverado Museum** (⊠ 1490 Library La., ☎ 707/963–3757), which contains manuscripts and memorabilia detailing the life of former resident Robert Louis Stevenson.

Continue north to woodsy **Calistoga,** a bastion of hot springs and spas offering every facial and body treatment under the sun—from mud baths to foot reflexology to herbal wraps. All the spas here are ostensibly gay-friendly. Many lesbian and gay San Franciscans simmer away their ills at **Indian Springs** (⊠ 1712 Lincoln Ave., ☎ 707/942–4913). **Lavender Hill Spa** (⊠ 1015 Foothill Blvd., ☎ 707/942–4495), south of town, is known for its seaweed wraps and aromatherapy.

The queerest of the bunch, though, is **Harbin Hot Springs** (⊠ Harbin Springs Rd.; take Hwy. 29 north, and then turn left on Hwy. 175, and right on Barnes St., which becomes Harbin Springs Rd., ☎ 707/987–2477), about 30 miles north of Calistoga above Middletown. Run by the groovy New Age Heart of Consciousness Church, Harbin provides the full gamut of treatments and has pools where you can shed your clothes as well as your tensions. There's also a small vegetarian restaurant. Accommodations cost a fraction of those at neighboring places, but here's the catch: Rooms are extremely drab and you're required to bring your own sheets.

For a look into the Calistoga's past, visit the **Sharpsteen Museum** (⊠ 1311 Washington St., ☎ 707/942–5911), a cottage filled with dioramas, exhibits, and memorabilia, much of it collected by the noted Walt Disney Studio animator Ben Sharpsteen. A highlight here is the material on author Robert Louis Stevenson, who once lived in these parts. Another popular attraction is **Old Faithful Geyser** (⊠ 1299 Tubbs La., Calistoga, ☎ 707/942–6463), which blows its top about every 40 minutes or so (most of the time).

Wineries

Some advice about tasting. Napa Valley is no longer the land of free wine; count on chalking up a nominal fee to sample a few vintages. In Sonoma, there are still many free tastings, but this is slowly changing. Also, wineries sell their stock at retail, often for 10% to 20% more than what you'll pay at your liquor superstore back home.

The list of wineries below is by no means comprehensive, but includes some renowned labels, places that offer fun or informative tours, and ones with attractive grounds where you can picnic before or after you taste.

Sonoma Valley

Vintners these days are constantly thinking up new ways to stand out. The folks at **Benziger** (⌧ 1883 London Ranch Rd., Glen Ellen, ☎ 707/935–4046) have accomplished this by offering an interactive tram tour, during which you'll be regaled with the ins and outs of modern-day wine making.

Count Agoston Haraszthy's 1857 **Buena Vista Carneros** (⌧ 18000 Old Winery Rd., Sonoma, ☎ 707/938–1266) is steeped in history; the art-filled, ivy-coated visitors center is impressive, and there's a picnic area. Unfortunately, since the 1989 Loma Prieta earthquake visitors have only been able to peer into the site's 19th-century wine caves.

In Kenwood, just north of Sonoma, the imposing 1920 Spanish-style mansion at **Chateau St. Jean** (⌧ 8555 Sonoma Hwy., ☎ 707/833–4134) anchors a 250-acre vineyard estate. The wines produced here happen to be some of the region's finest, but even nontasters may wish to stop by and survey the glorious grounds.

With its steady rise to stardom, Geyserville's **Clos de Bois** (⌧ 19410 Geyserville Ave., ☎ 707/857–3100) becomes crowded at times, but it's a pleasant excuse to wander through this charming little town.

Famous for its award-winning fumé blanc, **Dry Creek** (⌧ 3770 Lambert Bridge Rd., Healdsburg, ☎ 707/433–1000) has magnolia- and redwood-studded grounds.

Glen Ellen (⌧ 14301 Arnold Dr., Glen Ellen, ☎ 707/939–6277) is set inside a converted 19th-century gristmill.

A producer of one of the state's most popular chardonnays, **Kendall-Jackson** (⌧ 337 Healdsburg Ave., ☎ 707/433–7102) is a Healdsburg favorite.

Kunde (⌧ 10155 Hwy. 12, Kenwood, ☎ 707/833–5501), where the staff explains the entire wine-making process, is ideal for first-timers.

Napa Valley

The century-old **Beaulieu Vineyard** (⌧ 1960 S. St. Helena Hwy., Rutherford, ☎ 707/967–5230), which is set on Rutherford's glorious town square, was recently renovated. BV serves wine fit for a queen—Queen Elizabeth has tasted, for instance.

Beringer (⊠ 2000 Main St., St. Helena, ☎ 707/963–4812) has been around for more than 120 years, having survived Prohibition by producing communion wines. Be sure to tour the 1883 Rhein-style confection in which the winery is housed.

Come to **Clos Pegase** (⊠ 1060 Dunaweal La., Calistoga, ☎ 707/942–4981) as much to take in Michael Graves's innovative postmodern architecture and the extensive sculpture garden and modern-art collection as to sample the wines.

Fans of the bubbly shouldn't miss **Domaine Chandon** (⊠ 1 California Dr., Yountville, ☎ 707/944–2280), a cousin of French champagne producer Möet et Chandon. Domaine's restaurant is one of the swankest in the valley, but equally well-prepared fare can be had for less elsewhere.

Tours at Oakville's **Robert Mondavi** (⊠ 7801 St. Helena Hwy., ☎ 707/259–9463) are a big production, lasting from one to four hours.

Mondavi also has a hand, along with famed French vintner Baron Philippe Rothschild, in **Opus One** (⊠ 7900 St. Helena Hwy., Oakville, ☎ 707/963–1979). You have to make an appointment to tour the spaceshiplike headquarters (designed by the team that came up with San Francisco's Transamerica Pyramid), but it's worth reserving a slot.

If the constant bombardment of epicurean goodies inspires you to go home and cook, visit **Rutherford Grove** (⊠ 1673 St. Helena Hwy., Rutherford, ☎ 707/963–0544). In addition to several varieties of wines, Rutherford produces delicious cold-pressed grape-seed oil, a less-fattening and cholesterol- and sodium-free alternative to olive oil that's been a staple of European kitchens for centuries. Try a splash yourself.

The most expansive wine caves in America are located below **Rutherford Hill** (⊠ 200 Rutherford Hill Rd., Rutherford, ☎ 707/963–7194), which is just up the road from Wine Country's fanciest resort, Auberge de Soleil.

Stag's Leap (⊠ 5766 Silverado Trail, Napa, ☎ 707/944–2020) produced the wine that put the Napa Valley on the enological map two decades ago, and it remains a star vintner. Its dashing grounds are set away from the hustle and bustle of Highway 29.

An aerial tram sweeps visitors up to the main buildings of the area's winery in the sky, **Sterling Vineyards** (⌧ 1111 Dunaweal La., Calistoga, ☎ 707/942–3344), which has one of the largest gift shops in the region.

Balloon and Train Rides

Hot-air ballooning over the Napa and Sonoma valleys has become a favored pastime. The best-known operator is **Napa Valley Balloons, Inc.** (⌧ Yountville, ☎ 707/944–0228 or 800/253–2224). The rides typically take place at dawn and last an hour or more; back on earth, you'll be feted with a champagne brunch.

The locals hate it, but the **Napa Valley Wine Train** (☎ 707/253–2111 or 800/427–4124), which departs from 1725 McKinstry Street in the town of Napa, offers a tasty gastronomical chug through the Napa Valley. Riding in restored 1917 Pullman railcars, you'll see 14 miles of vineyards while dining on Continental cuisine. The train doesn't stop at any wineries, so don't mistake this for a transportation alternative.

GETTING AROUND

You can zip up to the Russian River towns from San Francisco in about 90 minutes by car. Travel along U.S. 101 north through Santa Rosa, getting off at the River Road exit. Follow this west for about 30 minutes to reach Guerneville. The Wine Country is the same distance from San Francisco. Follow U.S. 101 north to Highway 37 east (just south of Novato), then head north on Highway 121, which will take you first to the base of the Sonoma Valley and then to the base of the Napa Valley.

The town of Sonoma is about an hour from Guerneville, Napa another 20 or 30 minutes. In the Wine Country, the main routes—highways 12, 121, and 29—are often jammed with traffic on weekends.

WHEN TO GO

Summer is without question high season in the Russian River and the Wine Country, but year-round there's plenty to do and see. The climate is pleasant most of the year, but the likelihood of heavy rains can make for a rough winter and early spring in Guerneville. The Wine Country is dryer and less prone to temperature shifts.

Seasonal Events

Several events are tied to the visiting gay and lesbian communities, but the liveliest weekend in western Sonoma County is the two-day **Russian River Jazz Festival** (☎ 707/869–3940) on the weekend after Labor Day. The **Sonoma County Lesbian, Gay, Bisexual Pride Parade and Celebration** (☎ 707/544–8773), held in June in Santa Rosa, draws many folks from the Russian River. **Women's Weekend** (☎ 707/869–9000 for camping and lodging reservations) has long been a big hit in Guerneville. Held in May and again in September, the event includes musical and comedy performances, a crafts fair, creative workshops, and massage.

EATS

The quality and style of dining Sonoma and Napa counties varies, but generally the farther east you travel the more sophisticated and costly the fare. The Russian River vicinity is characterized by affordable, often rustic burger and pasta houses. Until recently, even gay visitors didn't demand much in the way of San Francisco–influenced nouvelle cooking.

Some of the West Coast's top chefs have opened restaurants in eastern Sonoma County and the Napa Valley, recognizing that a world-class wine-producing region demands world-class dining (and prices). You can still eat well on a budget, though—don't overlook the plethora of affordable gourmet delicatessens, cheese shops, and bakeries.

Most restaurants in and around the Russian River have strong gay followings. Almost none in the Wine Country do; however, you're eating alongside a fairly hip crowd.

For price ranges, *see* the dining chart at the front of this guide.

Russian River Vicinity

$$–$$$ ✕ **River's End.** If you venture through Sonoma's coastal towns, try to time your visit to include lunch or dinner at this German-influenced haven on a bluff above where the Russian River empties into the Pacific. Depending on the season, your table will look out over seals or migrating birds. Menu highlights include medallions of venison with mushrooms and crayfish in peppered game sauce; seviche of octopus, scallops, and shrimp; and game dishes. This is an area brunch favorite. ✉ *Hwy. 1., Jenner,* ☎ *707/865–2484.*

$$–$$$ ✕ **Sweet's River Grill.** This center-of-town eatery is the closest Guerneville has to a see-and-be-seen restaurant. The prime people-watching is done from sidewalk tables. A recent change in ownership greatly improved the cuisine. Try the broiled halibut with roasted red pepper and lemon butter or the avocado seafood remoulade. Nice beer and wine selection. ✉ *16251 Main St., Guerneville,* ☎ *707/869–3383.*

$$–$$$ ✕ **Village Inn.** The restaurant at this 1910 resort, where parts of Bing Crosby's *Holiday Inn* were filmed, is cozy and romantic, with warm lighting and the ambience of an old New England tavern. Favorites from the American and Continental menu are quiche Florentine, deep-fried prawns, blackened red snapper, and pepper steak. ✉ *20822 River Blvd., Monte Rio,* ☎ *707/865–2304.*

$$ ✕ **Bagdad.** Owned by the same women who run the Bagdad Cafe in the Castro, this lesbian-popular restaurant overlooks a small golf course. Best bets include the chicken in a light champagne sauce and the warm goat-cheese salad. ✉ *19400 Hwy. 116, Monte Rio,* ☎ *707/865–2454.*

$$ ✕ **Burdon's.** This casual roadside restaurant a bit east of downtown Guerneville has been a Russian River standby for years. Expect dependable, old-fashioned Continental fare such as breast of chicken Dijon with a mustard-and-wine cream sauce and scallions; veal scallopine sautéed with mushrooms and a marsala wine demi-glace; and excellent steak, either 8-ounce filet mignon or 14-ounce New York strip. ✉ *15405 River Rd., Guerneville,* ☎ *707/869–2615.*

$$ ✕ **Chez Marie.** For perhaps the most romantic dinner setting in the Russian River valley, drive 10 minutes east from Guerneville to this storefront French bistro in itsy-bitsy Forestville. Behind dainty window valances are several small tables and a pair of bookshelves packed with old cookbooks. The women who run this place could write a book of their own about their hits-the-spot fare—scampi pesto, escargots, pâté de maison, and cassoulet with cannellini beans, confit of duck, and ham. ✉ *6675 Front St. (Hwy. 116), Forestville,* ☎ *707/887–7503.*

Eats ●
Bagdad, **10**
Breeze Inn
Bar-B-Q, **7**
Brew Moon, **4**
Burdon's, **8**
Coffee Bazaar, **6**
Fifes, **2**
The Hiding
Place, **9**
Mill Street Grill, **3**
Molly's, **1**
Sweet's River
Grill, **5**

Scenes ○
Bullpen, **5**
Fifes, **2**
The Hiding
Place, **6**
Molly's Country
Club, **1**
Rainbow Cattle
Company, **4**
Triple R, **3**

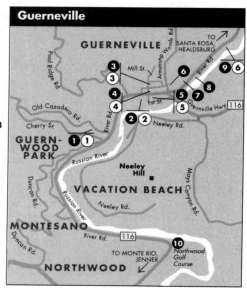

Guerneville

\$\$ ✕ **Fifes.** Brunch on the deck by the pool is a time-honored Russian River tradition at this gay resort. You can also have lunch or dinner inside or out. The American fare is okay—just okay—but the atmosphere is always saucy. ✉ *16467 River Rd., Guerneville,* ☎ *707/869-0656.*

\$\$ ✕ **Negri's Italian Dinners.** Tired of all the trendy creations being passed off as authentic Italian fare? For more than 60 years, Negri's has been serving family-style, no-nonsense northern Italian meals—shrimp, pasta, duck, and the like. The town's hungry he-male loggers were this place's first patrons: Expect enormous portions. ✉ *3700 Bohemian Hwy., Occidental,* ☎ *707/823-5301.*

\$-\$\$ ✕ **Breeze Inn Bar-B-Q.** Soon after you arrive in Guerneville you'll notice a peculiar three-wheel motorized vehicle zipping around town delivering slow-cooked pork ribs, smoked-salmon fillets, and barbecue chicken from the Breeze Inn. You can dine here, too. Vegetarians take heart: There are several options, including fettuccine or seasonal greens with corn-bread. The sweet-potato pie may topple you. ✉ *15640 River Rd., Guerneville,* ☎ *707/869-9208.*

$–$$ ✕ **Mill Street Grill.** The busy dining room at the Russian River Resort is one of the few places in the area that serves food after 10 PM (it's open until 4 AM). The traditional American food—pork chops, steak, eggs—isn't great, but the staff and crowd are friendly and fun-loving. ✉ *4th and Mill Sts., Guerneville,* ☎ *707/869–0691.*

$–$$ ✕ **Molly's.** The restaurant inside the gay country-western bar of the same name serves dinner late in the evening (until 10 on weekdays and 11 on weekends). Expect well-prepared chicken teriyaki and thick burgers—and plenty of queens in boots and jeans. ✉ *14120 Old Cazadero Rd., Guerneville,* ☎ *707/869–0511.*

$ ✕ **East West Cafe & Bakery.** If you've worked up an appetite antiquing in downtown Petaluma, satisfy your cravings at this quirky coffee and light-lunch spot. ✉ *128 N. Main St., Petaluma,* ☎ *707/829–2822.*

$ ✕ **The Hiding Place.** Saturday and Sunday mornings' walking wounded seek solace at this semi-outdoor roadhouse a short drive east of downtown. In addition to sandwiches and typical breakfast foods, you'll find some spicy Mexican fare—burritos, quesadillas, and the like. The two-tiered deck always catches a refreshing breeze. ✉ *15025 River Rd., Guerneville,* ☎ *707/869–2887.*

The Sonoma Wine Country

$$$$ ✕ **John Ash & Co.** Grapes from the surrounding 50-acre vineyard are used in this acclaimed restaurant's own chardonnay. On cool evenings dine by the fireplace; on warm ones sit on the patio. The seasonally changing menu might include sautéed Dungeness crab cakes with serrano mayonnaise, or grilled peppered-beef fillet with a port sauce and Gorgonzola cheese. ✉ *4330 Barnes Rd., Santa Rosa,* ☎ *707/527–7687.*

$$–$$$ ✕ **Lisa Hemenway's.** Run by a former chef at John Ash, this purveyor of things healthful never fails to deliver a fine meal. Savor skewered shiitake mushrooms with buckwheat noodles and a ginger sauce, or grilled sea bass with a piquant East Asian curry. The desserts are great, as are the box lunches at the Tote Cuisine Annex. ✉ *Montgomery Village, 714 Village Ct. Mall, Santa Rosa,* ☎ *707/526–5111.*

$$–$$$ ✕ **MIXX.** The menu of this star Railroad Square bistro is divided into small and large dishes. The smaller ones, ideal for group sampling, include smoked seafood and sweet-potato

Sonoma and Napa Counties

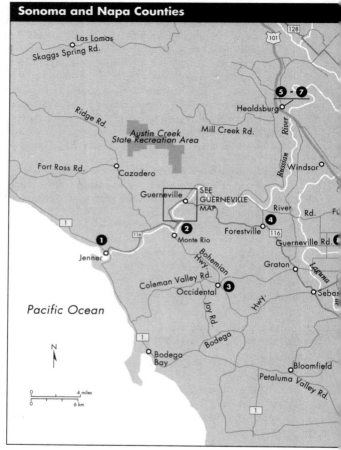

Las Lomas
Skaggs Spring Rd.

128
101

Ridge Rd.

⑤ · ⑦
Healdsburg

Mill Creek Rd.

Austin Creek
State Recreation Area

Russian River

Fort Ross Rd.

Cazadero

Windsor

Guerneville

SEE
GUERNEVILLE
MAP

River Rd.

④

Fu

116

②
Monte Rio

Forestville

Guerneville Rd.

①
Jenner

Bohemian Hwy.

Graton

Laguna

Coleman Valley Rd.

Occidental

③

Joy Rd.

Hwy.

Sebas

Pacific Ocean

N

Bodega

Bodega
Bay

Bloomfield

Petaluma Valley Rd.

0   4 miles
0   6 km

1

Eats ●

All Seasons Café, **13**	Chez Marie, **4**	Lo Spuntino, **22**	Stars Oakville Cafe, **16**
Auberge du Soleil, **15**	Domaine Chandon, **19**	Mangia Bene, **5**	Terra, **14**
Bistro Don Giovanni, **20**	East West Cafe & Bakery, **11**	MIXX, **10**	The French Laundry, **18**
Bistro Ralph, **6**	John Ash & Co., **9**	Mustards Grill, **17**	Village Inn, **2**
Brava Terrace, **21**	Lisa Hemenway's, **12**	Negri Italian Dinners, **3**	Willowside, **8**
		Ravenous, **7**	
		River's End, **1**	

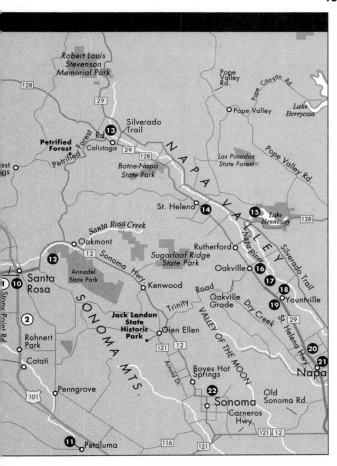

Scenes ○
Fun House, **1**
Santa Rosa Inn, **2**

gnocchi. One of the better full-size entrées is duck with grilled pears and warm noodle salad. Loud but fun, and open late on weekends. ⊠ *135 4th St., Santa Rosa,* ☎ *707/573–1344.*

$$–$$$ ✕ **Willowside.** When this rustic eatery opened a couple of years ago, every queer foodie in the region jumped for joy— finally, a restaurant in the woods (about 20 minutes east of Guerneville) worth salivating over. The short California-style menu changes often but might feature orzo with morels, ricotta, and radicchio, or perhaps coriander ahi tuna with similarly enticing accompaniments. You'll always find a few queens. ⊠ *3535 Guerneville Rd., Santa Rosa,* ☎ *707/523– 4814.*

$$ ✕ **Bistro Ralph.** Wine tasters pack into this informal bistro to partake of the outstanding California-style food—try the braised local lamb with a heady mint sauce—and to see what first-rate service is all about. Ask your server for advice about the Local Stash, the bistro's list of homegrown wines. ⊠ *109 Plaza St., Healdsburg,* ☎ *707/433–1380.*

$–$$ ✕ **Lo Spuntino.** On the corner of Sonoma's town green, this bright café is a quick and convenient detour for coffee, light salads (such as polenta with grilled squash, tomatoes, and red peppers), creative sandwiches, creamy gelato. ⊠ *400 1st St. E, Sonoma,* ☎ *707/935–5656.*

$–$$ ✕ **Mangia Bene.** This trattoria and pizza parlor is where Healdsburg locals catch up with each other and tourists can count on a trendily untrendy bowl of pasta after a long day of canoeing or wine tasting. ⊠ *241 Healdsburg Ave., Healds-burg,* ☎ *707/433–2340.*

$–$$ ✕ **Ravenous.** The restaurant beside the Raven, the last of Sonoma County's old-fashioned movie theaters, lives up to its mouthwatering name with robust burgers and hearty pastas. ⊠ *117 North St., Healdsburg,* ☎ *707/431–1770. No credit cards.*

The Napa Wine Country

$$$– ✕ **Terra.** The heavenly fare of this always-packed St. Helena
$$$$ favorite spans several regions: northern California, eastern Asia, and southern France to name a few. Hiro Stone is the former head chef of L.A.'s Spago, and his ingenious creations continue to dazzle. It's not every day that you find a menu with duck-liver wontons. Despite the high volume of diners,

an air of calm prevails. ⊠ *1345 Railroad Ave., St. Helena,* ☎ *707/963–8931.*

$$$ ✕ **Auberge du Soleil.** If *Ab Fab*'s Patsy and Eddie were to plunk themselves down anywhere in the Napa Valley, it would be over a table at this hilltop retreat above the Silverado Trail. Dishes like Thai-seared Hawaiian whole snapper and roasted lobster sausage dazzle the taste buds. The wooden deck overlooking the valley feels *très* Provençal, but the dining room is more evocative of Santa Fe, with a kiva oven and lodgepole pine ceilings. ⊠ *180 Rutherford Hill Rd., Rutherford,* ☎ *707/963–1211.*

$$–$$$ ✕ **All Seasons Café.** The perfect spot for a refreshing repast after a rejuvenating mud bath or massage, All Seasons has a remarkable wine list even by Napa standards, and outstanding regional dishes. The grilled lamb with fresh dill and the house-smoked salmon will wow you, and the staff will recommend the right vintage to go with your meal. ⊠ *1400 Lincoln Ave., Calistoga,* ☎ *707/942–9111.*

$$–$$$ ✕ **Bistro Don Giovanni.** This bistro is unflashy but consistently on the mark. The servers are light on their feet and the fare—thin-crust pizzas and delicate pastas—will keep you light on yours. Great vineyard views out the windows. ⊠ *4110 St. Helena Hwy., Napa,* ☎ *707/224–3300.*

$$–$$$ ✕ **Mustards Grill.** The definitive Wine Country restaurant, Mustards is presided over by Cindy Pawlcyn, who's also responsible for several other top-notch northern California eating spots, including nearby St. Helena's somewhat overrated Tra Vigne. You can eat well here without breaking the bank, sampling the spicy grilled-pepper appetizer filled with tamales and topped with tomatillo stuffing, or an entrée of roasted rabbit. ⊠ *7399 St. Helena Hwy., Napa,* ☎ *707/944–2424.*

In addition to the places reviewed above, you might consider these other Napa favorites: **Brava Terrace** (⊠ 3010 St. Helena Hwy. N, St. Helena, ☎ 707/963–9300; Cal French; $$$); **Domaine Chandon** (⊠ 1 California Dr., Yountville, ☎ 707/944–2892; nouvelle French; $$$$); **The French Laundry** (⊠ 6640 Washington St., Yountville, ☎ 707/944–2380; New American; $$$$); and **Stars Oakville Cafe** (⊠ 7848 St. Helena Hwy., Oakville, ☎ 707/944–8905; California cuisine; $$$), owned by San Fran restaurateur Jeremiah Tower.

Coffeehouse Culture

Aroma Roasters. This Railroad Square beanery at North Light Books (*see* Gay Media *in* The Little Black Book, *below*) draws a mix of alternateens, dykes with tykes, and tourists passing through. Very easygoing—a good place to get to know the locals. The bookstore has the region's best lesbigay selection. ✉ *95 5th St., Santa Rosa,* ☎ *707/579–9000.*

Brew Moon. One of the few Russian River spots that evokes a cosmopolitan air has an art gallery, recorded jazz, and such fanciful decorating elements as abstract murals, delicate glass tables, and colorful director's chairs. There's a light menu of sandwiches and sweets, plus an array of coffees. ✉ *16248 Main St., Guerneville,* ☎ *707/869–0201.*

Coffee Bazaar. With the steady trickle of beatnicky locals dropping by all day, a more apt name for this homey java joint might be the Coffee Bizarre. Excellent pastries. ✉ *14045 Armstrong Woods Rd., Guerneville,* ☎ *707/869–9706.*

SCENES

For a secluded community in the sticks, Guerneville serves up a varied nightlife scene. Nonguests are perfectly welcome to party at most resort bars. Several gay restaurants have taverns attached, and there are a couple of self-standing clubs. In summer places stay fairly crowded during the week and are packed on weekends. The rest of the year attendance tends to be sparse during the week and, unless there's a special event, on nonsummer weekends as well. Bars stop serving booze at 2, but many stay open later for dancing and hanging out. Women and men are welcome at all of the places listed, though the Triple R and Rainbow Cattle Company are mostly male.

PRIME SUSPECTS

Fifes. The bar and lounge at this resort were completely rebuilt—and elevated—following the '94–'95 floods. Now you head up a flight of stairs to the main tavern; a comfy rec room with large-screen TVs is off to the left. There's live piano music many nights. Out the back door and to the right the sprawling sundeck and pool area is always lively on weekend afternoons. ✉ *16467 River Rd.,* ☎ *707/869–0656. Crowd: 80/20 m/f, all ages but the youngest ones get there early in the day to work their tans.*

Molly's Country Club. This entertainment adjunct to the Western-style restaurant is run by the owners of the Highland Dell in Monte Rio. They took Guerneville by storm in 1996 by throwing a series of foam parties, for which the entire dance floor was filled waist-high with something akin to shaving cream. If you've never been to a foam party, dress scantily and plan to slip around—it's great fun unless you're claustrophobic or picky about who slides up against you. Most of the time this is a casual spot for two-stepping and line-dancing. ✉ *14120 Old Cazadero Rd.,* ☎ *707/869–0511. Crowd: 75/25 m/f, country-western fans.*

NEIGHBORHOOD HAUNTS

The Hiding Place (✉ 15025 River Rd., ☎ 707/869–2887) in eastern Guerneville is known mostly as a casual restaurant, but fags and dykes also come for cocktails, especially in the early evening. In 1996 Sweet's River Grill added a gay sports bar, the **Bullpen** (✉ 16251 Main St., ☎ 707/869–3383), which draws a loyal local crowd.

Rainbow Cattle Company (✉ 16220 Main St., ☎ 707/869–0206), a former gambling hall, draws a fairly butch gang of gay guys and some women, many of whom tumble in after 11 for a nightcap. Watch your hat, this place can get rowdy. A good stopover before hitting one of the River's larger clubs is the little video and piano bar at the **Triple R** (✉ 4th and Mill Sts., ☎ 707/869–0691), where the fireplace and several friendly bartenders keep everybody's spirits up. The crowd is mostly male, but women are very welcome.

There are no gay bars in the Wine Country; the closest you'll find is the **Santa Rosa Inn** (✉ 4302 Santa Rosa Ave., ☎ 707/584–0345), a saloon, dance hall, and piano bar on the outskirts of Santa Rosa, almost in Rohnert Park.

ONE NIGHTERS, MOVEABLE FETES

The usually straight **Fun House** (✉ Railroad Square, 120 5th St., Santa Rosa, ☎ 707/545–5483 or 707/545–1773), the largest disco in the northern Bay Area, becomes Club Heaven on Sundays and draws a mostly gay and lesbian crowd for dancing until 4 AM. This is a well-attended event; lots of Russian Riverites make the trip. On other nights you'll usually see a few same-sexers.

Action

Considering the number of bathhouses, sex clubs, and adult bookstores in the Bay Area, it's surprising that such things don't much exist in the Russian River. The resorts can get racy and cruisy, as can the public beaches along the Russian River, but there is no sleaze venue per se. **Santa Rosa Adult Books** (⊠ 3301 Santa Rosa Ave., Santa Rosa, ☎ 707/542–8248) is the nearest purveyor of porn.

SLEEPS

Accommodations in the Russian River towns of Guerneville and Monte Rio are not unreasonably priced, but those in the heart of the Wine Country can be costly. If you're looking for inexpensive motels, stick to Santa Rosa, which has dozens of affordable chain properties along Highway 12.

Russian River gay resorts bear little resemblance to the sleek, often luxurious gay getaways in Palm Springs. Some of the places in Guerneville and Monte Rio can be downright spare. The upside is that you also may fall asleep at night in front of a wood-burning stove while staring through redwoods at a starlit sky.

If you're interested in camping, you'll find sites at Fifes and the Willows (*see below*), and at the **Faerie Ring Campground** (⊠ 16747 Armstrong Woods Rd., Guerneville 95446, ☎ 707/869–2746) and **Schoolhouse Canyon** (⊠ 12600 River Rd., Guerneville 95446, ☎ 707/869–2311).

For price ranges, *see* the lodging chart at the front of this guide.

Hotels

The Wine Country

$$$ 🏨 **Doubletree Hotel.** There aren't many full-scale resorts in the Wine Country, but this hilltop retreat provides the privacy and anonymity that most smaller properties can't, and the management is gay-friendly. Rooms are spacious and have decks or balconies. ⊠ *3555 Round Barn Blvd., Santa Rosa 95401, ☎ 707/523–7555 or 800/222–8733, FAX 707/545–2807. 245 rooms. Restaurant, pool, fitness center.*

Guest Houses and Small Hotels

Russian River Vicinity

$$$–
$$$$ 🏨 **Applewood.** Friendly hosts Jim Caron and Darryl Notter, and their even friendlier dogs, greet guests at this posh miniresort a few minutes from downtown Guerneville. Half the rooms are in the main 1922 Mission Revival house; the others are in a recently built second building done in the same style. All are loaded with antiques and have European down comforters. Most rooms have French doors leading to balconies or shaded verandas. If you're celebrating an anniversary and can afford deluxe digs, this is your ultimate Russian River retreat. There's a restaurant attached that's open to nonguests on a space-available basis. Prix-fixe dinner menus change often, but might feature Tuscan roast chicken or grilled leg of lamb. ⊠ *13555 Hwy. 16, Pocket Canyon 95446,* ☎ *707/869–9093,* 🆇 *707/869–9170. 16 rooms with phone, TV, and private bath. Restaurant, pool, hot tub. Mixed gay/straight.*

$$$ 🏨 **Huckleberry Springs.** You'll discover plenty of elbow room at this 56-acre tree-studded resort that's high on a hill above the Russian River. Huckleberry Springs has four cottages, each with a skylight and a wood-burning stove. The secluded retreat is just a 10-minute drive from the bars and restaurants of Guerneville. The folks here serve a terrific full breakfast and offer a range of massage therapies. For an extra $25, guests can partake in a first-rate three-course dinner. ⊠ *Box 400, Monte Rio 95462,* ☎ *707/865–2683 or 800/822–2683. 4 cottages with private bath. Restaurant, pool, hot tub. Full breakfast. Mixed gay/straight.*

$$–$$$ 🏨 **Fern Grove Inn.** Here you'll find the most luxurious accommodations in Guerneville proper. The main inn and several Craftsman-style cottages all date from the mid-'20s, and there are two newer villas. Rooms have private entrances, decks, knotty-pine-paneled walls, and a mix of antiques and contemporary pieces; many have fireplaces and VCRs (there's an on-site film library). Not much of a party place, the inn is ideal for couples. ⊠ *16650 River Rd., Guerneville 95446,* ☎ *707/869–9083 or 800/347–9083. 22 units with TV and private bath. Pool. Continental breakfast. Mixed gay/straight.*

$$–$$$ 🏨 **Highland Dell Inn.** The chalets of Germany's Black Forest were the inspiration for this top-notch 1906 inn. The Highland Dell was largely remodeled after the torrential rains of

'95 but retains a warm mix of Victorian and 20th-century antiques in the guest rooms and public areas. Most of the leaded and stained glass, as well as a magnificent wooden chandelier, survived the flood, and such new amenities as automated voice mail have been added to every room. (For a fuller idea of what to expect from the inn—at least in terms of decor—check out Falcon Video's scintillating *By Invitation Only*, which was filmed on the premises.) The full breakfast is elaborate and filling. The Highland Dell was hit hard again by the '97 flood, but hosts Glenn Dixon and Anthony Patchett remain dedicated to keeping their inn open. ✉ *21050 River Blvd., Monte Rio 95462, ☎ 707/865–1759 or 800/767–1759. 10 rooms with phone and private bath. Full breakfast. Mixed gay/straight.*

$$ 🛏 **Paradise Cove.** Rooms at this peaceful compound a mile north of downtown Guerneville are unfancy but receive plenty of natural light and have wooden decks with views of rhododendron, passion flowers, and other native plants. Most have cozy wood-burning stoves, and there's an extremely pleasant pool and deck area. ✉ *14711 Armstrong Woods Rd., Guerneville 95446, ☎ 707/869–2706 or 800/880–2706. 15 rooms with private bath, most with TV. Pool, hot tub. Continental breakfast. Mostly gay male.*

$$ 🛏 **Rio Villa.** This complex of green and white cabins is perched on the banks of the Russian River just a short walk from the bridge in Monte Rio. The cabins have been recently remodeled; most have private decks and outdoor grills. Herb and flower gardens accent the well-kept grounds, and there's easy beach access. A very good value overall. ✉ *20292 Hwy. 116, Monte Rio 95462, ☎ 707/865–1143, FAX 707/865–0115. 14 units with TV and private bath. Continental breakfast on weekends. Mixed gay/straight.*

$–$$ 🛏 **Fifes.** This is the quintessential rustic resort; it's also the largest gay compound in the region, with a restaurant and bar. Cabins and cottages are simple, but many have wood-burning stoves and wet bars. There are also several dozen campsites, and guests can roam through the property's 15 acres of rose gardens and wooded trails. The many on-site facilities and activities include a private beach, a sprawling pool and sundeck, a small gym, volleyball, and canoeing. ✉ *16467 River Rd., Guerneville 95446, ☎ 707/869–0656 or*

800/734–3371. *52 cabins with TV and private bath. Restaurant, pool, hot tub, exercise room. Mixed gay male/lesbian.*

$–$$ ⊡ **Highlands.** Modest and low-key, this 4-acre gay resort is a short walk from downtown. Nudity is permitted around the pool and hot tub. Some rooms have kitchens, and there are also cabins with fireplaces. A nice value. ⊠ *14000 Woodland Dr., Guerneville 95446,* ☎ *707/869–0333. 16 rooms, many with private bath. Pool, hot tub. Continental breakfast on weekends. Mixed gay male/lesbian.*

$–$$ ⊡ **The Russian River Resort.** The "Triple R" has a devoted following of guys. The motel-style rooms are small, clean, and affordable; some have wood-burning fireplaces. ⊠ *4th and Mill Sts., Guerneville 95446,* ☎ *707/869–0691 or 800/417–3767. 23 rooms with TV; many have private bath. Restaurant, pool, hot tub. Mostly gay male.*

$–$$ ⊡ **The Willows.** This secluded resort with a sprawling old country lodge and a 60-site tent-and-RV campground sits right on the edge of the Russian River, nestled amid groves of pine and willow trees. Guest rooms in the lodge have dark-wood paneling and VCRs. A homey common room has a fireplace and a grand piano. Use the inn's paddleboats and canoes or laze along the beach or on the sundeck. An excellent value. ⊠ *15905 River Rd., Guerneville 95446,* ☎ *707/869–2824 or 800/953–2828. 13 rooms with phone and TV, 9 with private bath. Hot tub. Continental breakfast. Mixed gay male/lesbian.*

The Wine Country

$$$$ ⊡ **Auberge du Soleil.** The choice of foreign dignitaries, San Fran yupsters, and other money's-no-object sorts, Auberge is a discreet retreat. Rooms have a Tuscan-meets-southwestern sensibility, with warm earthy hues, tile fireplaces, and private terraces overlooking the miles of vineyards and orchards below. Each room is equipped with a CD player, a stereo, and a VCR. Skin and body treatments are available, including aloe and aroma wraps, shiatsu massage, and ayurveda therapy, an ancient detoxifying treatment. ⊠ *180 Rutherford Hill Rd., Rutherford 94573,* ☎ *707/963–1211 or 800/348–5406,* FAX *707/963–8764. 48 rooms with phone, TV, and private bath. Restaurant, pool. Mostly straight.*

$$$–$$$$ ⊡ **Villa Messina.** This stately 1986 mansion is modeled after an Italian villa and sits high on a slope with panoramic views of Mt. St. Helena and Mt. Alexander from just about every room. One of the common rooms contains an enormous saltwater aquarium filled with exotic fish, and all public and guest rooms are loaded with art, antiques, and deco furnishings. Rooms have VCRs, and one has a fireplace and double Jacuzzi. ⊠ *316 Burgundy Rd., Healdsburg 95448,* ☎ *707/433–6655,* ℻ *707/433–4515. 5 rooms with phone, TV, and bath. Pool, hot tub. Full breakfast. Mixed gay/straight.*

$$$ 🏨 **Madrona Manor.** With its striking mansard roof, pointed dormer windows, and sweeping wraparound porch, this imposing three-story 1881 mansion looks like the ideal setting for a Gothic horror movie. Many of the Madrona's antiques, including a rosewood square grand piano, are original to the house, which has been run as an inn since the early 1980s by Carol and John Muir. The main house holds nine rooms, with another 12 among the outbuildings. The restaurant features dishes such as smoked lamb salad, Dungeness crab mousse, and over-roasted pork tenderloin. ⊠ *1001 Westside Rd., Healdsburg 95448,* ☎ *707/433–4231 or 800/258–4003. 21 rooms with phone and private bath. Restaurant, pool. Full breakfast. Mixed gay/straight.*

$$–$$$ 🏨 **Camellia Inn.** One of the Wine Country's finest Italianate Victorian houses is run like a first-rate small hotel. Innkeepers Del and Ray Lewand are warm hosts, and they've filled the inn and its two outbuildings—one a cleverly restored water tower with two guest rooms—with Oriental rugs and eclectic antiques. More than 50 varieties of picture-perfect camellias lace the premises. ⊠ *211 North St., Healdsburg 95448,* ☎ *707/433–8182 or 800/727–8182,* ℻ *707/433–8130. 10 rooms, most with private bath. Pool. Full breakfast. Mixed gay/straight.*

$$–$$$ 🏨 **El Dorado Hotel.** With the absence of any specifically gay-popular accommodations in Sonoma, you might consider this small 1840s hotel on the town plaza. Rooms have tile floors, goose-down comforters, balconies, and rustic furnishings—they're simple and quite tasteful. ⊠ *405 1st St. W, Sonoma 95476,* ☎ *707/996–2351 or 800/289–3031. 27 rooms with phone, TV, and private bath. Restaurant, pool. Mostly straight.*

$$–$$$ 🏨 **Ink House Bed & Breakfast.** One of the few sanctuaries of comfort and elegance along otherwise noisy and busy Highway 29 has remained very popular with lesbians and gays since Diane Horkheimer purchased it in late 1995. Rooms have high ceilings and many antiques, and the fourth-story belvedere that crowns the yellow 1884 Italianate house yields panoramic Napa Valley views. Room rates include a filling hot breakfast and evening wine and hors d'oeuvres. ⊠ *1575 St. Helena Hwy., St. Helena 94574,* ☎ *707/963–3890. 7 rooms, 5 with private bath. Full breakfast. Mostly straight.*

$$ 🏠 **Twin Towers River Ranch.** A group looking to spend a weekend or more in the Wine Country isn't likely to find a more gay-friendly option than the two unique homes on the property adjoining this B&B, presided over by innkeepers Bill and Marty. The unusual Redwood Tree House, which sleeps up to 10 and practically touches the Russian River, is built around five 250- to 300-foot trees. You enter it through a 200-year-old redwood. Another redwood, around which the kitchen is built, is 6 feet in diameter. More traditional and intimate, the 1863 Oak Tree House sleeps three couples and has a private beach. The inn itself, a sprawling 1863 ranch house, holds two antiques-filled rooms. Both have balconies overlooking the property's 500-foot beach. ⊠ *615 Bailhache Ave., Healdsburg 95448,* ☎ *707/433–4443. 2 rooms with private bath, 2 furnished homes. Continental breakfast for B&B guests. Mixed gay/straight.*

THE LITTLE BLACK BOOK

At Your Fingertips

Healdsburg Area Chamber of Commerce (⊠ 217 Healdsburg Ave., 95448, ☎ 707/433–6935). **Napa Valley Visitors Bureau** (⊠ 1310 Napa Town Center, Napa 94559, ☎ 707/226–7459). **Russian River Chamber of Commerce** (⊠ 16200 1st St., Guerneville 95446, ☎ 707/869–9000). **Russian River Visitors Center** (⊠ 14034 Armstrong Woods Rd., Guerneville 95446, ☎ 707/869–9212). **Santa Rosa Chamber of Commerce and Convention and Visitors Bureau** (⊠ 637 1st St., 95404, ☎ 707/545–1414 or 800/404–7673). **Sonoma County Convention & Visitors Bureau** (⊠ 5000 Roberts Lake Rd., Suite A, Rohnert Park 94928, ☎ 707/586–8100). **Sonoma Valley Visitors Center** (⊠ 453 1st St. E, Sonoma 95476, ☎ 707/996–1090).

Gay Media

We The People (⊠ Box 8218, Santa Rosa 95407, no phone) is the gay-and-lesbian monthly newspaper serving the Russian River and Wine Country.

BOOKSTORES

There's no gay bookstore in Guerneville, but the **River Reader** (⊠ 16355 Main St., ☎ 707/869–2240) is a small independent store with a decent lesbian-and-gay section and an idiosyncratic selection of mainstream titles. Santa Rosa's **North Light Books** (⊠ Railroad Sq., 95 5th St., ☎ 707/579–9000), an excellent mainstream independent, has a fine lesbigay selection. Also on the premises is the gay-friendly coffeehouse Aroma Roasters. **Ariadne Books** (⊠ 3780 Bel Aire Plaza, Napa, ☎ 707/253–9402) is another mainstream bookstore with a lesbigay section and a coffee bar.

5 Out in Monterey Bay

THE MONTEREY PENINSULA IS ONE of coastal California's favorite weekend getaways. Too far from San Francisco for a day trip, most visitors also find it too limited in diversions for a lengthy stay; it's ideal for a two- to four-day excursion, however. Gay and lesbian travelers will find little here that speaks specifically to them, though most locals describe the peninsula as tolerant on social issues and generally laid-back. The queer population is substantial, but it's not exactly high-profile, and there's no gay district. Monterey had its first gay-pride parade in 1996, and the same year a mostly lesbian bar opened across the street from Monterey's long-running queer club, After Dark. Monterey is a discreet, WASPy place; fitting in here is less a matter of sexual orientation than of apparent socioeconomic status.

Santa Cruz shares few traits with the upscale and straight-laced Monterey Peninsula, save for breathtaking views over Monterey Bay. The city has an anachronistic edge; it brings the '60s into the '90s without the least sense of irony. The city remains ratty on the surface despite random attempts at gentrification—yes, those are two-dozen Krishnas in floral-print gowns chanting, dancing, and waving tambourines outside a Gap store. Many say the area is slowly declining to the point of seediness. Others read the spate of rebuilding since the 1989 Loma Prieta earthquake (which was centered near here) as a sign that things are back on the right track.

What's undeniable about Santa Cruz is its great philosophical and spiritual diversity. The city is a hub of New Age and Eastern religious practice. It also has the most cohesive and visible feminist and lesbian community in California, more so even than San Francisco's or Berkeley's.

THE LAY OF THE LAND

The cities of Santa Cruz and Monterey occupy the opposite
ends of a 50-mile crescent of coastline. At the southern tip,
Monterey, Pacific Grove, Pebble Beach, and Carmel sit on a
small peninsula that juts into the Pacific. Below here begins
the dramatic portion of Highway 1 that hugs the rocky coast
south through Big Sur, San Simeon, Cambria, and Morro Bay
before heading on to Santa Barbara.

Monterey

The handful of blocks around north–south-running Alvarado
Street and the perpendicular Del Monte Avenue form Monterey's downtown, a comparatively dull neighborhood except for a few good restaurants and several historic houses.

To get a feel for area history, stop by the **Monterey State Historic Park Visitor Center** (⊠ 5 Custom House Plaza, ☎ 408/
649–7118). It's housed inside the Monterey Maritime Museum, which overlooks the bay at the northern end of downtown. The park contains many historic structures, a few of
them 19th-century adobes. You can take guided tours (they
depart three times daily from the visitor center), or explore
the buildings yourself; just pick up the park's "Path of History" brochure.

The adjacent **Monterey Maritime Museum** (☎ 408/375–
2553) and nearby **Custom House** (⊠ 1 Custom House Plaza,
☎ 408/649–2909) document Monterey's history as a sea-
trading port. The 1827 Custom House, the oldest govern-
mental building on the West Coast, is one of the state historic
park's most engaging components.

Robert Louis Stevenson lived briefly in the south end of
downtown in a cheap hotel, now called **Stevenson House** (⊠
530 Houston St., ☎ 408/649–7118). You'll find many of his
personal belongings inside. A couple of blocks west a 1929
Mediterranean-inspired former train station houses the **Monterey Peninsula Museum of Art** (⊠ 559 Pacific St., ☎
408/372–7591), whose strengths include photography and
folk art. Even more impressive is the museum's newer branch,
La Mirada (⊠ 720 Via Mirada, ☎ 408/372–3689), housed
in a 19th-century adobe east of downtown on Fremont
Street. La Mirada holds European and Asian antiques, as well
as a fine collection of Californian and Asian art.

Like San Francisco, Monterey has a touristy and basically uninteresting **Fisherman's Wharf,** this one a few hundred feet west of the Custom House. Continue west to reach the equally touristy but somewhat more engaging **Cannery Row.** John Steinbeck's novel of the same name depicted this once-gritty heart of America's sardine-fishing industry. Overexploitation during the middle of this century resulted in a huge drop in the sardine catch. The canneries closed and years later were transformed into the restaurants, shops, and amusements of today.

Some of this, including a wax museum and many chain establishments, is reprehensibly commercial. One imagines that the spirit of John Steinbeck is little moved by the wharfside shopping plaza erected in his honor. If you're willing to endure crowds, do visit the **Monterey Bay Aquarium** (⌧ 886 Cannery Row, ☎ 408/648–4888), which is as impressive as any you'll ever lay eyes on. The aquarium was expanded in 1996; its new million-gallon indoor ocean reportedly contains the largest window in the world. Also worth a browse is the 130-dealer **Cannery Row Antique Mall** (⌧ 471 Wave St., ☎ 408/655–0264).

Monterey is an excellent place for blading and biking, watching sailboats in the bay, and admiring the backdrop of green mountains. There's no better spot to enjoy these pastimes than at the western flank of **Shoreline Park,** which begins at the aquarium and extends into the neighboring and far less commercial town of **Pacific Grove,** where it eventually becomes **Hayes Perkins Park.** At the foot of 10th Street you'll find **Lovers Point;** several benches here rest on an outcropping above the surf. At night you and your special someone can sit below a small canopy of cypress trees and a higher one of stars, discovering ways to take the chill off Monterey's brisk sea breezes (this is by no means a cruisy park, so bring your own lover).

Colorful Victorians and contemporary bungalows dominate the peaceful neighborhood surrounding Lovers Point. To the west the **Pacific Grove Museum of Natural History** (⌧ Forest and Central Aves., ☎ 408/648–3116) has exhibits on local wildlife, plants, and geology, along with information about the town's famed November–March monarch-butterfly migration. **Point Piños Lighthouse** (☎ 408/648–3116), which can be toured on weekends, is the focal point of Pacific

Grove's northwest corner; **Asilomar State Beach,** south of the lighthouse, is a fine stretch of sand.

To golfers **Pebble Beach,** just below Pacific Grove, is America's answer to the Royal & Ancient in St. Andrews, Scotland. For years the most prestigious, nonmajor PGA golf tournament, the AT&T Pro-Am (formerly named for its early master of ceremonies, crooner Bing Crosby), has revolved around Pebble Beach's windswept links. For a stiff fee ($100–$250) you can try your luck on one of several courses with gnarled cypress trees—and hope your ball doesn't plop into the frothy sea below. A less athletic challenge involves driving the tortuous **17-Mile Drive,** which affords views of the coastline's spectacular outcroppings, not to mention scads of harbor seals and sea lions. It may seem ridiculous to fork over $6.50 for the privilege of a seaside drive, but it's worth it—and it's certainly cheaper than a round of golf.

Carmel

Downtown Monterey is ordinary, but little **Carmel** is an enchanting pine- and cypress-shaded maze of upscale boutiques and gingerbread-style cottages that variously evokes Swiss-alpine, coastal-Mediterranean, and country-English hamlets. The town's location on a hill atop one of the most scenic beaches along the California coastline only enhances the picture-book atmosphere. The downside, not surprisingly, is that the town's popularity has far outstretched its ability to manage the swarms of pedestrians and cars. Parking is nearly impossible downtown or at the beach on weekends.

Ocean Avenue, which leads down to the beach, is the main shopping drag. Traditional and fairly cutting-edge galleries occupy many of the storefronts, along with a goodly number of jewelry shops—art or gem collectors will not be disappointed. Amid the boutiques is one midsize mall, **Carmel Plaza** (⊠ Ocean Ave. and Junipero St.), that holds about 50 shops. Outdoorsy types may wish to visit **Birkenstock Footprints** (⊠ 6th Ave. and San Carlos St., ☎ 408/624–5779), the nation's first store to specialize in the comfy sandals.

Carmel began as one of Father Junípero Serra's late-18th-century missions. The **Carmel Mission** (⊠ Rio Rd. and Lasuen Dr., ☎ 408/624–3600) is one of the best-preserved such compounds, with a stern-looking stone church, dense gardens of poppies, and a fascinating old library.

You can tour poet Robinson Jeffers's **Tor House** (⊠ 26304 Ocean View Ave., ☎ 408/624–1813), which balances precariously on the tip of a jagged promontory above the Pacific. Filled with art, books, and many of Jeffers's collectibles, it makes for a highly entertaining visit.

Below town are two of the region's most precious natural resources. **Carmel River State Park** (☎ 408/624–4909), a birdwatching paradise off Highway 1, has more than 100 acres of forests, dunes, and estuaries. The 456-acre **Point Lobos State Reserve** (⊠ Hwy. 1, ☎ 408/624–4909), an outstanding hiking park that's also favored by scuba divers, is an excellent place for a picnic. Inland several miles, Carmel Valley Road hugs the banks of the Carmel River, leading into a fertile region of agriculture and winemaking.

Santa Cruz

The downtown of this city of 50,000 is a direction-defying tangle of crooked, often one-way, streets. The scythe-shaped San Lorenzo River slices through the maze; most of the commercial activity is west of it.

Pacific Avenue is a groovy strip of record shops, bookstores, coffeehouses, and various cerebral diversions from about Water Street to Laurel Street. Pacific Avenue manifests the city's multiple personalities. Alongside derelict lots vacant since the '89 earthquake are cosmopolitan new restaurants, and shops proffering exotic gemstones and tapes of wailing loons; lip-pierced, purple-haired boys glide lithely by on skateboards. The city's one gay bar is here. On summer Saturdays tanned kids from the burbs cruise the avenue in shiny red Jeeps blaring hip hop or grunge. The dominant facial expression of the many down-and-out-looking genXers is one of intense boredom. Members of Santa Cruz's new citizens patrol walk stiffly through the throng of slackers, arousing charges of Orwellian vigilantism from the city's libertarian core. Pacific Avenue is many things, but it is not dull.

You'll discover a whole different Santa Cruz along the harbor at the south end of downtown. Just east of the intersection of Cliff Drive and Beach Street, seafood shanties and souvenir stands line the long **Municipal Wharf.** The charmingly faded **Boardwalk** (☎ 408/423–5590) has been central to Santa Cruz's image since 1906; its half-mile-long wooden roller coaster, the Giant Dipper, began getting a rise out of tourists in 1923. The Looff carousel was built in 1911. Not all the 25 rides are worth the price of admission, but there's no charge to roam amid the corn-dog stands and T-shirt booths. The spiffy grand ballroom of the old **Cocoanut Grove** still lands top-name performers. Some in Santa Cruz feel that the Boardwalk has become seedy in recent years, hence the introduction of the citizens patrol.

Cultural institutions in town include the small **Museum of Art and History at the McPherson Center** (✉ 705 Front St., ☎ 408/454–0697), which exhibits regional contemporary art and artifacts that explore the social history of Santa Cruz. The **Santa Cruz City Museum of Natural History** (✉ 1305 E. Cliff Dr., ☎ 408/429–3773) on the east bank of the San Lorenzo River includes displays on local geology and animal life. Underwhelming even if you're into the sport is the **Surfing Museum** (✉ Lighthouse Point, W. Cliff Dr., ☎ 408/429–3429). For some views of Monterey Bay follow West Cliff Drive from downtown for a couple of miles as it curves along the rocks above the surf.

Santa Cruz is a major center of New Age practice and philosophy, and the town is home to a number of lesbian- and gay-frequented spas. One truly worth checking out is **Well Within** (✉ 417 Cedar St., ☎ 408/458–9355), which has a private hot tub and sauna suites, and trained massage therapists. The peaceful establishment overlooks a Japanese garden.

The campus of the **University of California Santa Cruz (UCSC)** sprawls across the evergreen- and redwood-studded hills northwest of town. Established in 1965, this is the most unconventional institution in the state's university system; classes are not graded but critiqued, and every manner of social, labor, and political injustice is challenged both in and out of the classroom. The school has a vocal and organized queer community, one defined more by its political sensibilities than any concept so mundane as sexual orientation. If you stop by the cheap restaurants or shops on Highway 1 below campus, you'll find scores of fliers announcing upcoming readings, meetings, and rallies, some of them gay-related. And you'll get a real feel for the school by considering the tone of the classifieds. A typical request: "Wanted, lesbian, nonsmoking, vegan roommate to share with four cats and a chinchilla."

Signs on Mission Street (Highway 1) point the way to UCSC. Dense foliage blocks out the buildings, and several parking areas lead to hiking trails. Strong on performing arts and lecture series (☎ 408/459–2778 for information), the school presents a nationally acclaimed Shakespeare festival (☎ 408/459–4168) each summer.

If the weather's fair and you're up for a breathtaking excursion, head north from Santa Cruz on Highway 1 for about 7 miles. On your right you'll pass Laguna Road; continue another ⅛ mile and you'll reach a second Laguna Road (they used to be connected in the shape of a horseshoe). Park in the small dirt lot. The trailhead to **Laguna Creek Beach** is directly across busy Highway 1. Follow the trail over train tracks, along a grassy plateau, and down a short but steep hill to the secluded cove below. The surf is loud and wild and the wind can be strong, but there are several sheltered spots along the base of the cliffs where you can throw down a blanket. Nudity is common here. Note that there's no parking in the lot from 10 PM to 6 AM.

A scenic way to return to Santa Cruz from here is to continue north on Highway 1 for about a mile from where you parked. Turn right onto Bonny Doon Road. Follow this up a steep hill roughly another mile and make a right onto Smith Grade. At some point, pull over, get out, and smell the evergreens and wildflowers—the hills are infused with their aroma. Smith Grade winds through a thick forest, at some points becoming a one-lane road. It eventually ends at the intersection with Empire Grade, onto which a right turn will lead you back to the UCSC campus.

GETTING AROUND

From San Francisco it's about a two-hour drive to Santa Cruz and a three-hour drive to Monterey. Exceptions are summer Friday evenings and weekends, when traffic slows, often dramatically. The scenic route is along Highway 1, which fringes the coast. The drive is pleasant, though not as spectacular as it is along other parts of California's central and northern coasts. You might consider taking Highway 1 one way, and in the other direction using the faster interior route—I–280 to Highway 17 below San Jose (or the reverse).

City streets in this region are not difficult to navigate. The problems arise when you attempt to park. Finding spaces near Santa Cruz's beach and pier on sunny weekends can be a chore. Finding parking on almost any afternoon in downtown Carmel or around Cannery Row in Monterey can also be tough. Perseverance will usually yield a spot, though sometimes you'll have to spring for a garage or a lot.

WHEN TO GO

Santa Cruz and the Monterey Peninsula are year-round destinations, with summer the peak season for tourists. Although it's frequently foggy and windy around Monterey, it's generally temperate year-round. Usually sunny and mild Santa Cruz is less susceptible to dampness, but can also be windy. In early June, you might come to see the **Santa Cruz Lesbian, Gay, Bisexual, Transgendered Pride Celebration** (☎ 408/425–5422). In 1996 Monterey began holding its **pride march** (☎ 408/647–8234), typically a week or two before San Francisco's. Santa Cruz has an impressive **Blues Festival** (☎ 408/479–1854) in late May and a **County Fair** in mid-September (☎ 408/724–5671).

EATS

The Monterey Peninsula has the more expensive and sophisticated dining scene, but Santa Cruz offers a broader range of cooking styles. Restaurants in Monterey and Carmel specialize in the bistro- and trattoria-inspired fare found in the Wine Country, though with a greater emphasis on seafood. Santa Cruz cuisine exhibits some of these influences, but there's also a wealth inexpensive ethnic and vegetarian restaurants and some funky sandwich shops and burger stands. Both communities have plenty of Mexican and Southwest eateries.

Gay-popular establishments don't really exist around Monterey—not even the waitrons down here are queens! Where else in California can you find a trendy dining scene with nary a gay or lesbian maitre d'—let alone plate clearer—in sight? Santa Cruz, in contrast, has at least a dozen spots with decidedly gay or at least left-leaning crowds. The alternative-minded hangouts on Highway 1 near UCSC's campus are almost all gay-friendly, as are the ones along Pacific Avenue downtown. Though in general Santa Cruz is the mellower place to dine, class and taste come into play as well. A couple of same-sexers in sweaters and khakis might receive a warmer welcome at a straight Monterey oyster bar than in some unionized Santa Cruz tofu shanty with Che Guevera memorabilia on the walls and pink triangles in the window. Go figure.

For price ranges, *see* the dining chart at the front of this guide.

Monterey Peninsula

$$$–
$$$$

✕ **Old Bath House.** If romance matters, the peninsula is without a better setting for a special dinner. A converted 1930s bathhouse (no, not *that* kind) overlooks Lovers Point and the surf below, and the food lives up to the ambience in every way. The menu changes often and spotlights local ingredients; you might start with artichoke heart and Havarti ravioli covered with a lemon-nutmeg cream sauce, and continue with pan-roasted pork medallions paired with candied Maui onions and sour cherries. ⊠ *620 Ocean View Blvd., Pacific Grove,* ☎ *408/375–5195.*

$$$

✕ **Montrio.** This restaurant set inside a restored brick building is simply outstanding. The service is always on the ball, and the chef turns out everything from dependable rotisserie chicken to more elaborate dishes like a caramelized onion tart with thyme chevre and black olives, and an oven-roasted portobello mushroom polenta with a ragout of grilled vegetables. Desserts are also amazing (the lemon angel food cake is a favorite) at this establishment run by the fabulously successful owners of Tarpy's Road House and the Rio Grill. ⊠ *414 Calle Principal, Monterey,* ☎ *408/648–8880.*

$$$

✕ **Tarpy's Road House.** Lest you associate Monterey dining solely with ocean views, Tarpy's is inland on a wooded hillside, set inside an ivy-covered ranch house attached to the highly regarded Ventana Vineyards. Dine inside or out; there's no way not to find a great table. The kitchen is fond of oak grilling—among the standouts are the turkey breast with roasted-garlic mashed potatoes and the bourbon-molasses pork chops. ⊠ *Hwy. 68, at Canyon Del Rey near the airport, Monterey,* ☎ *408/647–1444.*

$$–$$$

✕ **Piatti.** Murals of rosemary, eggplants, Parmesan cheese, and other enticing provisions enliven Piatti's terra-cotta tile-floor dining room, from which you can watch the chefs in

152

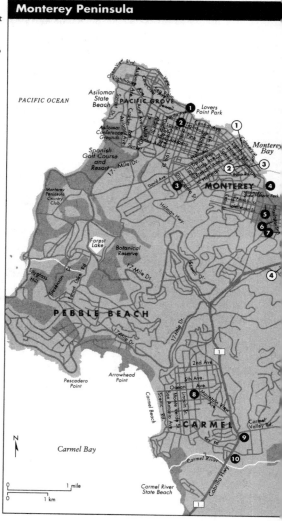

Monterey Peninsula

the open kitchen prepare such specialties as oak-grilled piz-zas, rotisserie chicken, and pasta. ⊠ *6th and Junipero Sts., Carmel,* ☎ *408/625–1766.*

$$–$$$ ✕ **Rio Grill.** Although it's away from downtown Carmel in a shopping center, the Rio Grill is one of the region's long-time favorites for southwestern-influenced New American food. The entrées—healthful grilled meats and poultry (in-cluding great burgers)—are fine, but the kitchen excels with smaller dishes such as the warm goat cheese with a roasted pasilla pepper–walnut pesto and the refried chipotle-mint black beans. Faux-adobe accents and earth tones make for a se-date main dining room, but you can also eat in the bar, where an amazing array of celeb caricatures covers the walls. Only drawback: pokey service. ⊠ *Crossroads Shopping Cen-ter, Hwy. 1 and Rio Rd., Carmel,* ☎ *408/625–5436.*

$$ ✕ **Cafe Fina.** Area gays patronize this café, the best of Mon-terey's seaside eateries, the perfect place to try fresh seafood, including grilled Petrale sole, steamed clams, blackened-snapper salad, and crab ravioli. There are plenty of steak and veal dishes, too, in case you left your sea legs at home. In a hurry? Grab a slice of brick-oven pizza to go. ⊠ *Fisherman's Wharf, Monterey,* ☎ *408/372–5200.*

$$ ✕ **Clock Garden.** No restaurant in Monterey is overwhelm-ingly queer, but the Clock Garden probably has the strongest gay following. The best seats are in a garden with a foun-tain, a fire pit, hanging terra-cotta lamps, and flowers ev-erywhere. Ribs, roasted chicken, burgers, pastas, and "Welsch rabbit" (muffins, sherry, bacon bits, salad) are among the fill-ing fare. The wine selection is impressive, and the crème brulée for dessert is a local hit. A big scene for Sunday brunch. ⊠ *565 Abrego St., Monterey,* ☎ *408/375–6100.*

$–$$ ✕ **Allegro Gourmet Pizza.** Many believe these places serve the best pizza in the Monterey Bay area. Stellar pies include one with separate sections of salami, artichokes, mushrooms, and anchovies, and another with Gorgonzola, fontina, mozzarella, and Parmesan cheeses topped with roasted red peppers and pistachio nuts. ⊠ *1184 Forest Ave., Monterey,* ☎ *408/373–5656;* ⊠ *3770 The Barnyard, Carmel,* ☎ *408/626–5454.*

Santa Cruz

$$–$$$ ✕ **Clouds Downtown.** Contemporary, airy, and rather sleek for Santa Cruz's funky downtown streetscape, this wine bar is one of the town's top purveyors of California and Pacific Rim cooking. Ahi tuna carpaccio with soy, wasabi, and pickled ginger works quite well, as does the fresh rabbit with applewood-smoked bacon and corn-and-wild-rice pancakes. ⊠ *110 Church St.,* ☎ *408/429–2000.*

$$ ✕ **Cooper Street Cafe.** A hip little study in brass and glass serves tasty international fare and presents live jazz on weekends. In fine weather you can sit in the courtyard on black and tan director's chairs. Feta-stuffed chicken and roasted tri-tip steak are a couple of the better entrées; there's also lighter fare, ranging from quiche to soups and fresh-baked bread. ⊠ *725 Front St.,* ☎ *408/423–4925.*

$$ ✕ **Gabriella.** Romantic and affordable, this cozy downtown cottage serves home-style Italian dishes. The pastas, risottos, and pizzas (try the one with sweet Italian sausage, mushrooms, and garlic) are great, as are such light salads as white beans over arugula and radicchio, topped with herbs and olive oil. ⊠ *910 Cedar St.,* ☎ *408/457–1677.*

$$ ✕ **India Joze.** Set inside the Santa Cruz Art Center is a restaurant, bakery, coffeehouse, and gallery all in one. The menu might feature your choice of calamari, lean lamb, or strips of chicken stir-fried in a Persian pomegranate, mint, and cream sauce; or Javanese basil-tamarind-ginger pesto wokked with red snapper, tofu, or pasta with prawns. Most other dishes also utilize this mix-and-match formula. ⊠ *1001 Center St.,* ☎ *408/427–3554.*

$–$$ ✕ **Crêpe Place.** For 25 years this jazzy little creperie inside a tin-roof Victorian house has been a friend to the gay community. Crepes both sweet and savory are served in an antiques-filled dining room and a garden courtyard. Salsa crepes are filled with avocado, cheese, onions, green chilies, and tomatoes; another favorite has smoked salmon. This is one of the few spots to grab a bite as late as midnight (1 AM on weekends). ⊠ *1134 Soquel Ave.,* ☎ *408/429–6994.*

$–$$ ✕ **Positively Front Street.** Downing large quantities of seafood near the wharf is a Santa Cruz tradition, and most locals agree that this rollicking place a half block from the wharf serves the best crab cakes, steamed clams, and stuffed mushrooms. ⊠ *44 Front St.,* ☎ *408/426–1944.*

$–$$ ✕ **Szechwan Garden.** The inexpensive downtown lunch and dinner spot serves excellent vegetarian dishes such as broccoli with a tangy ginger-garlic sauce. ⊠ *617 Pacific Ave.,* ☎ *408/423–2574.*

$ ✕ **Herland Cafe.** This intimate café attached to the feminist bookstore of the same name specializes in vegetarian and vegan

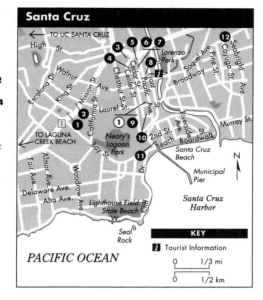

Eats ●
Cafe Brazil, **1**
Clouds Downtown, **7**
Cooper Street Cafe, **8**
Crêpe Place, **12**
Gabriella, **6**
Herland Cafe, **4**
India Joze, **3**
Pacific Avenue Pizza, **5**
Positively Front Street, **11**
Saturn Cafe, **2**
Szechwan Garden, **10**
Zachary's, **9**

Scenes ○
Blue Lagoon, **1**

Map title: **Santa Cruz**

Map labels: TO UC SANTA CRUZ; High St.; Escalona Dr.; Walnut; King St.; Mission St. Ave.; California St.; Chestnut St.; Cedar St.; Center St.; Front; Pacific Ave.; Lorenzo Park; Broadway; Soquel Ave.; Pine St.; Cayuga St.; Seabright Ave.; Laurel St.; Neary's Lagoon Park; TO LAGUNA CREEK BEACH; Bay St.; Almar Ave.; Fair Ave.; Woodrow Ave.; Delaware Ave.; Alta Ave.; 2nd St.; Beach; Riverside Ave.; Boardwalk; Murray St.; Santa Cruz Beach; Municipal Pier; Santa Cruz Harbor; Lighthouse Field State Beach; Cliff Dr.; Seal Rock; PACIFIC OCEAN; N

KEY
i Tourist Information
0   1/3 mi
0   1/2 km

dishes—sandwiches, organic salads, soups, hot casseroles, and the like. Women who are new in town will find this an excellent place to make friends and learn of upcoming events. ⊠ *902 Center St.,* ☎ *408/429–6641.*

$ ✗ **Pacific Avenue Pizza.** Typical pizzas on this casual parlor's menu are interspersed with some unusual ones, such as the green chilies and Louisiana-style hot sausage pie. You can also try the sourdough pizza sandwich, an open-face creation with tomato sauce, cheese, and your choice of three or four toppings. ⊠ *1415 Pacific Ave.,* ☎ *408/425–7492.*

$ ✗ **Saturn Cafe.** This place could be the prototype for funky, neosocialist collegiate cafés with its mismatched chairs, shaggy plants, old lamps, a pint-size disco ball, and UCSC students engrossed in deep political discourses. The food is crunchy and quirky; typical is the alien sandwich, with tofu, hummus, avocado, and cheese. You'll also find a good selection of soups and salads. The bathrooms are painted silver and have planetary murals—a lovely touch. Open till midnight. ⊠ *1230 Mission St.,* ☎ *408/429–8505. No credit cards.*

$ ✕ **Zachary's.** The brunching choice of Santa Cruz's queer
community is a simple storefront near the Blue Lagoon nightclub. The usual sandwiches and egg dishes are available, but
the baked goods—jalapeño corn bread, sourdough pancakes,
cream-cheese scones—earn the bravos. ⊠ *819 Pacific Ave.,*
☎ *408/427–0646.*

Coffeehouse Culture

Although there are quite a few of them in Monterey, including a fairly artsy one inside **Bay Books** (*see* Gay Media
in The Little Black Book, *below*), coffeehouses here are not
the sort of gay and lesbian social centers that they are elsewhere. One that has developed something of a queer reputation, particularly among women, is **Wildberries** (⊠ 212 17th
St., Pacific Grove, ☎ 408/644–9836).

Many restaurants including **Herland Cafe, India Joze,** and
the **Cooper Street Cafe** (*see above*) double as espresso bars;
there are also chain coffeehouses along Pacific Avenue.

Cafe Brasil. It's easy to meet UCSC fags and dykes at this
ramshackle place—grab some lit crit, have a seat, and see who
pops over to say hello. Of course, with so many skate-
boarders zipping through, it's hard to keep track of everybody. ⊠ *1410 Mission St.,* ☎ *408/429–1855.*

SCENES

Monterey Peninsula

After Dark/Back Lot. If you need proof that Monterey is a
straight-laced town, note that in this place it's usually the handful of heteros with the pierced ears and tattoos, not the
homos. You'll find a snazzy little cocktail bar up front and
beyond that a small dance floor with a fine sound system and
lighting. In back is the club's best feature, a landscaped,
two-tier deck with wooden benches and a fire pit. Behind this
is another even dressier cocktail bar called the Back Lot. The
staff is polite and outgoing, and the patrons seem always to
be enjoying themselves immensely. ⊠ *214 Lighthouse Ave.,*
☎ *408/373–7828. Crowd: 70/30 m/f, guppie, collared shirts
and Bermuda shorts, Ann Taylor dykes, approachable, unpretentious but a tad cliquey.*

Tidal 9. Given the strength of the Monterey Bay area's lesbian population, it's surprising that it took until 1996 for a full-time dyke bar to open. What's even more surprising is that it opened in Monterey, not Santa Cruz. The tavern bills itself as a women's sports bar but is open to anybody. One room has a pair of pool tables, plus darts and other games. Another has video screens, including a 35-inch TV on which NFL games are broadcast throughout the fall. There's a small dance floor, and the management brings in local DJs. The bar serves munchies and gourmet pizzas. ⊠ *281 Lighthouse Ave.,* ☎ *408/373–4488. Crowd: 70/30 f/m plus straight friends of the community, sports buffs, mostly 30s and 40s types, mixed butch and guppie, very friendly.*

Elsewhere on the Monterey Peninsula are oodles of straight yuppie bars. One spot with a slightly gay following, **Planet Gemini** (⊠ 625 Cannery Row, ☎ 408/373–1449), presents rock bands, comedians, and other big-name acts.

Near Monterey

Franco's Norma Jean. If you're a fan of Marilyn Monroe, drag, small-town queer bars, or simply curious sights, consider hopping over to mellow Castroville, a little dot on the map between Monterey and Santa Cruz that's earned its fame by producing an annual bumper crop of artichokes. Campy almost to the point of being Twilight Zonish, Franco's is packed with Marilyn paraphernalia, from movie posters to photos to Franklin Mint statuary. It's only open on Fridays, when the crowd is mostly lesbian, and Saturdays, when a wild drag show is staged around midnight. The first Saturday in June is your chance to enter a Marilyn Monroe drag-alike pageant. There's a small dance floor, a boutique selling MM memorabilia, and a '50s-style diner serving such dishes as the MM burger, which is topped with Swiss cheese and some of Castroville's prized artichoke hearts. Franco has used his establishment to raise a tremendous amount of money for charity. ⊠ *10639 Merritt St., Castroville,* ☎ *408/633–2090. Crowd: all over the map.*

Santa Cruz

Blue Lagoon. This three-room club in the heart of downtown is the only place in Santa Cruz with a dance floor, so it's been a source of controversy that more straights have been showing up lately, especially on weekends throughout the college year. You have to think more about who's who and who to cruise, but the crowd is generally liberal. The best room is the quasi-lounge with three pool tables and funky booths above which hang Keith Haring prints. There's a smaller bar up front; the dance floor in back has a small stage. ✉ *923 Pacific Ave.,* ☎ *408/423–7117. Crowd: 65/35 m/f, some straights, liberal and funky, leftist collegiates, graying Birkenstock types, few stand-and-model types, politically correct.*

Action

Bathhouses and gay adult bookstores are not part of the Monterey Bay landscape. Santa Cruz's **Laguna Creek Beach** (*see* The Lay of the Land, *above*) can be cruisy, but meeting somebody here is by no means guaranteed.

SLEEPS

Accommodations in Monterey vary from bare-bones strip motels to historic hotels. Pacific Grove just might be the B&B capital of the Central Coast, Pebble Beach is home to a pair of world-class golf-and-tennis resorts, and Carmel has a mix of resorts and upscale inns. Generally, the farther south you go the more expensive your options. Santa Cruz has cheap chain and independent motels, but lacks a first-rate full-service hotel. Fortunately, the handful of small inns nearby are charming and well run.

As for gay-specific accommodations, it's amazing that not a single guest house in the region caters to gay men and lesbians or even has a particularly strong following. The mainstream inns reviewed below are all hospitable, but at none are you especially likely to run into other same-sex couples. One property just south of Santa Cruz, **The Grove** (*see below*), rents two separate cottages to women.

Women who are comfortable staying in a private house might consider the **Misty Tiger** (☎ 408/633–8808; $$). Its owners, Angie and Jody, rent a large bedroom with a private bath. Guests have use of a long porch, secluded yard, and hot tub outside; inside you can settle in front of the fireplace in the game room or pick out a tape from the film library and laze away in front of the VCR. In Santa Cruz, **Ravenswood** (☎ 408/476–5742; $$) is a sprawling house with one room for rent on 5 acres overlooking Monterey Bay.

For price ranges, *see* the lodging chart at the front of this guide.

Hotels and Motels

Monterey Peninsula

$$$$ 🖩 **Inn at Spanish Bay.** Not as historic as the famed Lodge at Pebble Beach, the Inn at Spanish Bay nevertheless promises more pampering, better-equipped rooms, and the same access to the Pebble Beach golf and sports facilities. This stunning spread is just off 17-Mile Drive, overlooking Monterey Bay. Rooms have patios or balconies and gas fireplaces. The crowd is straight and conservative, worth braving if you'd like to stay in one of the country's top resorts. ⊠ *2700 17-Mile Dr., Pebble Beach 93953,* ☎ *408/647–7500 or 800/654–9300,* 𝖥𝖠𝖷 *408/644–7955. 270 rooms. Restaurant, pool, health club.*

$$$–
$$$$ 🖩 **Monterey Plaza Hotel.** This posh Mediterranean-style hotel is set partially on pilings in the bay, thus affording maritime vistas and quick access to a long sandy beach. Rooms have quality reproduction antiques, and many have balconies on the water. The Duck Club restaurant wows guests with stellar California cuisine. ⊠ *400 Cannery Row, Monterey 93940,* ☎ *408/646–1700 or 800/631–1339,* 𝖥𝖠𝖷 *408/646–0285. 285 rooms. Restaurant, exercise room.*

$ 🖩 **Monterey Downtown Travelodge.** Clean and cheap, this no-frills motel is a short drive from Monterey attractions and close to Highway 1, which makes for easy access in and out of town. ⊠ *675 Munras Ave., Monterey 93940,* ☎ *408/373–1876 or 800/578–7878,* 𝖥𝖠𝖷 *408/373–8693. 49 rooms. Pool.*

Santa Cruz

$ 🖩 **Candlelite Inn.** Of the endless supply of interchangeable motels downtown, this family-run property is one of the best. The staff is welcoming, the rooms are clean and large, and if you're looking for peace and privacy, the suites in the rear of the property are perfect—and still not very expensive. ⊠ *1101 Ocean St., 95060,* ☎ *408/427–1616,* 𝖥𝖠𝖷 *408/427–9053. 42 rooms. Restaurant, pool.*

$ 🖩 **Sunset Inn.** This peaceful no-frills motel on Highway 1 by the University is only a short drive from the beach. Here you won't have to deal with the downtown crowds. ⊠ *2424 Mission St., 95060,* ☎𝖥𝖠𝖷 *408/423–3471. 28 rooms.*

Guest Houses and Small Hotels

Monterey Peninsula

$$$ ⌂ **Cobblestone Inn.** A former motel was masterfully converted into a regal inn with stone fireplaces, English country antiques, homey quilts, and a refined atmosphere. ⌧ *8th and Junipero Aves., Box 3185, Carmel 93921,* ☎ *408/625–5222 or 800/833–8836,* FAX *408/625–0478. 24 rooms with phone, TV, and bath. Continental breakfast. Mostly straight.*

$$–$$$ ⌂ **Cypress Inn.** Part-owned by Doris Day, this white Moorish-influenced Mediterranean inn has attractive if not fancy rooms. Day, a prominent animal-rights campaigner, made this one of the few area inns to accept pets. ⌧ *Lincoln St. and 7th Ave., Box Y, Carmel 93921,* ☎ *408/624–3871 or 800/ 443–7443,* FAX *408/624–8216. 34 rooms with phone, TV, and bath. Full breakfast. Mostly straight.*

$$–$$$ ⌂ **Gosby House.** In the heart of downtown Pacific Grove, this turreted Queen Anne is filled with Victorian antiques and reproductions. Many rooms in the former boardinghouse have fireplaces. Although it's straight-owned, the inn has long had a following among gays and lesbians. ⌧ *643 Lighthouse Ave., Pacific Grove 93950,* ☎ *408/375–1287 or 800/527–8828,* FAX *408/655–9621. 22 rooms with phone, most with private bath. Full breakfast. Mixed gay/straight.*

$$–$$$ ⌂ **Green Gables.** One of Pacific Grove's most striking Queen Annes is a perfect specimen. Most rooms have three-sided bay windows with ocean views. For more space choose a room in the carriage house. ⌧ *104 5th St., Pacific Grove 93950,* ☎ *408/375–2095,* FAX *408/375–5437. 11 rooms, 9 with private bath. Full breakfast. Mostly straight.*

$$ ⌂ **Monterey Fireside Lodge.** This 20-year-old complex is near downtown close to several chain hotels. Rooms are spacious and have pleasant resort furnishings; about half have fireplaces. The owners have long marketed to gays and lesbians. ⌧ *1130 10th St., Monterey 93940,* ☎ *408/373–4172,* FAX *408/655–5640. 24 rooms with phone, TV, and bath. Hot tub. Continental breakfast. Mixed gay/straight.*

Santa Cruz

$$$ ⌂ **Inn at Depot Hill.** One of the most captivating properties in the Monterey Bay area, this elegant inn—whose rooms are named and styled after memorable European cities and villages—is fashioned out of a late-19th-century former train depot. ⌧ *250 Monterey Ave., Capitola 95010,* ☎ *408/462–*

3376 or 800/572–2632, ☐ 408/462–3694. 8 rooms with phone, TV, and bath. Full breakfast. Mostly straight.

$$ ☷ **The Grove.** Actually in the quiet community of La Selva in southern Santa Cruz County, this women-only artists' minifarm consists of two fully furnished cottages in a secluded spot overlooking Monterey Bay. ☐ *Call for address,* ☎ *408/ 724–3459. 2 cottages with bathrooms, 1 with TV. Hot tub. Women only.*

THE LITTLE BLACK BOOK

At Your Fingertips

Equinox (☐ 903 Pacific Ave., Santa Cruz, ☎ 408/457–1441; a community resource for gay and bisexual men under 30). **Monterey County AIDS Project** (☎ 408/394–4747). **Monterey Peninsula Chamber of Commerce** (☐ 380 Alvarado St., Monterey, 93942, ☎ 408/649–1770). **Santa Cruz AIDS Project** (☎ 408/427–3900). **Santa Cruz County Convention and Visitors Council** (☐ 701 Front St., Santa Cruz 95060, ☎ 408/425–1234 or 800/833–3494). **Santa Cruz Lesbian, Gay, Bisexual, and Transgendered Community Center** (☐ 1328 Commerce La., ☎ 408/425–5422). **Santa Cruz Women's Health Center** (☎ 408/427–3500). **UCSC Gay, Lesbian, Bisexual, and Transgender Resource Center** (☎ 408/459–2468).

Gay Media

Monterey's gay community is served by **The Paper** (☎ 408/655–3756), which comes out every two months. A comprehensive source for local arts and entertainment news is **The Herald** (☎ 408/372–8401).

The lesbian and gay **Lavender Reader** (☎ 408/423–8044), a quarterly magazine, carries interviews, fiction, editorials, and local news; it's well written and designed. **Good Times** (☎ 408/458–1100) and **Metro Santa Cruz** (☎ 408/457–9000) are arts-and-entertainment weeklies.

BOOKSTORES

Bay Books (☐ 316 Alvarado St., ☎ 408/375–1855) in downtown Monterey stocks a small queer section. **Bookshop Santa Cruz** (☐ 1520 Pacific Ave., ☎ 408/423–0900) has an excellent lesbigay selection. Also try **Herland Book and Cafe** (☐ 902 Center St., ☎ 408/429–6641) and **Logos** (☐ 1117 Pacific Ave., ☎ 408/427–5100).

INDEX

× = restaurant, ⊡ = hotel